I Am Church

Converting Passion into Praise

Daniel Holder

WESTBOW
PRESS®
A DIVISION OF THOMAS NELSON
& ZONDERVAN

WestBow Press books may be ordered through booksellers or by contacting:

WestBow Press
A Division of Thomas Nelson & Zondervan
1663 Liberty Drive
Bloomington, IN 47403
www.westbowpress.com
1 (866) 928-1240

ISBN: 978-1-9736-2599-5 (sc)
ISBN: 978-1-9736-2600-8 (hc)
ISBN: 978-1-9736-2598-8 (e)

Library of Congress Control Number: 2018904515

Print information available on the last page.

WestBow Press rev. date: 5/4/2018

Acknowledgments

To God: I am forever grateful that you chose me. I pray and work to be faithful in the use of my talents.

To my wife, Salina: Thank you for choosing me to be the recipient of your love, prayers, and immense support. None of the changes in my life would have been possible without you. This book is a symbol of what your love makes possible.

To my daughters, Abigail and Grace: Thank you for allowing me to be your dad, and loving me, even though I've never done this before. You two have been the catalyst for my growth. I look forward to watching you grow into the powerful women of God I know you will become. I want you to be as proud of me as I am of my father.

To my father, Pastor Richard Holder: You inspired me to write this book. You gave me permission to be different and showed me that with sweat and effort, dreams can come true.

To my mother, Pennie Holder: In your own special way, you encouraged me to continue working. You gave me my love for studying the bible and reading. Without you and my father to talk to, I am constantly reminded that the time in my life for talking is over.

are renouncing their belief in Christianity. People are leaving their Christian faith behind because Christians have not backed up words with action. We wear "What Would Jesus Do?" bracelets, but still do things that Jesus would not do, without repentance. The people leaving are our friends, our brothers, and sisters. They are our family, and you don't just let family leave.

It is time for a rebranding of Christianity. The church still has the responsibility of showing the world Jesus, but churches are not buildings. Churches are people. We are the church. The church was created to show the world Jesus. The biggest misconception of church is that church is a building, but that is not true. If you want to see what God's church looks like I suggest that you head over to a mirror. Church buildings were made by men, and some of them are lavish and beautiful. God's church was handcrafted by God and is perfect. God's church is you!

The purpose of this book is not to convince anyone who doesn't attend church to attend or to discourage anyone from attending church. In fact, I encourage regular church attendance, but if you don't want to go to church, you may find ways to become the church. Now, this may seem like a far-fetched idea, but it is quite simple. You behave like you'd want to see others behave. You be the model of Jesus that you desire to see other Christians be. The purpose of this book is to encourage you to be the church to the people you interact with on a daily basis. Be a church that makes an impact on your community and your world. Be the salt of the earth and be the light of the world. Don't worry; I'll help you to make sense of this as you read on.

Attending church should be a part of the journey that leads you closer to God. This is known as discipleship. Unfortunately, it is too easy to attend a church and remain the same person. Fortunately, the discipleship journey is not exclusive to church. This journey is made by examining the life of Jesus. After examining and modeling the life of Jesus, your behavior and life perspective should change.

Your daily action should be intentional. My goal is that you can turn what you are passionate about into praise. By praise, I don't mean praise and worship music. I mean something that people encounter and are drawn closer to God. As we draw others closer to God, God will draw us. As you read, I will show you how I've seen miraculous changes in my life.

Do you belong to a traditional church family but wonder how a bigger impact could be made on your community? Do you sometimes wonder how your church could be a greater agent of change in social and community issues? How can we make traditional church less about church politics and more about action? How can we make the church building a place of growth, not repetition? If any of these questions spark your interest, then you and I are in one accord. In an environment where resources are diminishing and needs are increasing, I often wonder how we can do church more effectively. My dad used to tell me, "If you want something done right, do it yourself." The responsibility to make an impact in this world is in our hands.

This book is my reaction to what I've seen in the church since I've been a part of one. Fortunately, I'm not old enough to accept things the way that they are when it comes to my active faith. I still believe I can change my world, and because you are still reading, I know you believe you can too. I wrote this book because I want to help others experience Jesus. I believe by guiding souls to God, the world can be and will be a better place. Even those who may not consider Jesus to be God cannot deny his historical impact. His purpose was to change our world. No other leader was and is as influential than Jesus. Today, he has over 2.2 billion followers, over 2000 years after his death and resurrection. Countless organizations model his leadership techniques. Jesus was one person who gathered twelve followers (disciples) and taught them to lead. And because of him, we can do this same thing.

The purpose of this portion of this book is to invoke conscious thought and to initiate a needed conversation. I do not want you to read this book and think about others. I want you to consider yourself and what you can do to be more impactful in your beliefs and actions as a believer. We all have unique strengths that we can tap into to help connect the church with what is relevant to the world today. The key to making this connection is to grow spiritually. Focusing on spiritual health is a great component of bridging the gap between the church and the world. Change starts from within.

Jesus once said, "Destroy this temple and in three days I will raise it up."[1] Jesus knew that he was the church and that he was responsible for representing his Father. Today, I want you to understand that you too are the church. Being the church involves connecting with people and being aware of their problems. This means that everything you do must align with the bigger purpose. Ministry is connecting people with God, and it doesn't just happen in the church; it happens through the church. It happens when you and I operate in it. We cannot leave ministry solely up to the church building and those who inhabit it. We have to share in the ultimate responsibility of being disciples of Jesus by acting in love at all times. In doing this, we assume our rightful positions as church.

---

[1] John 2:19

Chapter One
Call Me Jonah

all me Jonah. Well, my real name is Daniel Holder, but I liken a part of my life to the story of Jonah. You may be familiar with Jonah's story from when you were a child; but just in case you are not, Jonah was a prophet of God. He ran from doing God's work and in turn, God led a giant fish to swallow him up. After this, of course, Jonah did what God told him to do.

God's message for Nineveh was not hindered by Jonah's stubbornness and disobedience. In fact, Jonah's disobedience led him exactly where he needed to be. Jonah's stubbornness enhanced his message. Jonah's disobedience, at least to me, was the most spectacular part of this story. The sailors questioned him, and he said, "I serve the Lord who created the sea and the land." The men knew the Lord, so they were afraid. Jonah told them to throw him into the sea, because the storm was his fault. Can you imagine throwing a man into a stormy sea? Jonah surrendered to these strangers and allowed them to toss him overboard. He didn't jump; they threw him overboard and the sea calmed immediately. The sailors witnessed the power of God that day, something they may have never encountered had they not met Jonah or listened to him when he told them to toss him into the sea.

Nothing brings out passion like a near death experience. What would have happened if God had given this assignment to an obedient prophet? Jonah's disobedience was no surprise to God. It was a part of his journey. This assignment was not only about Nineveh; it was about Jonah. We all have a journey and some of us may have a Jonah story…like I do.

The PK Effect

PKs get a bad rep. Oh, "PK" stands for "preacher's kids." Many people have said that the children of preachers are often the worst behaved. In my case, those stereotypes may have been correct. I knew how to play the church game. A neat outfit and a smile was all that was required. I was known as the "good" son while my brother was the "crazy" son. One day, as my dad, Pastor Richard Holder, finished his sermon, he walked out of church to see my brother in handcuffs on a cop car. I'm sure people from church thought my brother was crazy. My brother is not crazy; he is a talented entrepreneur,[2] he just had a bad day. But this perception of who he is still remains. After all, isn't that what traditional church is about?

My Jonah experience began when my parents sent me from London, England, to Huntsville, Alabama. My mother wanted me to be a pastor like my father. I chose to major in accounting. I would have chosen any career over being a pastor. My mother told me that she'd be praying for me to change my mind. I told her, "Keep praying!" And pray she did! My journey didn't involve a giant fish, but it did involve lots of questionable decision making. My college experience involved a fraternity, heavy drinking, near death experiences, lots of fights, and an arrest. At the same time, I gained lots of work experience. I worked as a hotel manager, a plumber, and started a

---

[2] www.sophisticatedknots.com

career as a project manager in the U.S. Air Force. Now I've done a full circle. I'm studying for ministry. I guess Mother's prayers work.

As I am now accepting that God has a purpose for my life, I desire to bring my experiences and my passion to ministry. I am adamant about introducing innovation into ministry to help the world see and feel results when it comes to faith. Currently, church primarily focuses on the service on one day, in one location. I want to encourage Christians to think about how to serve God every day, not just one day out of the week. We must work together as one body to serve God. Church should grow us through connecting us with people and with God. After attending a church service or gathering, we should be able to see our progress. Growth does not happen with one day of work. Spiritual and relational growth is what I want to see happen in the church and for the church. The word discipleship refers to following another. In the case of Christianity, it refers to following Jesus. When you follow Jesus, you will see changes in your life. I believe that serving God for six days a week, rather than the focus on the one, is how to see these changes. I believe in the urgency of this message. I need to see a change in me sooner than later. Focusing on Christianity for six days rather that one would bring about that change much faster. Doing this would require prayer, consistent communication, and a sense of community.

Life has taught me that God can take our ordinary talents and make use of them to change the world. The lives we live play testament to the power of God. Your life is ministry and is the biggest sermon anyone will ever see. You are not a Christian because you attend church or because you return a tithe. You are a Christian because of your connection with Jesus and your ministry to others. Currently, I don't have a church building, but my family and I are the church because we serve others on a daily basis. My wife, Salina, and my two beautiful daughters, Abigail and Grace, work alongside me in doing the work of ministry. We seek to extend our spiritual family by being the Christians we need to be to spark change in the world. We serve faithfully for no other reason than loving God and loving his people.

My name is Daniel, but I am Jonah. My mother always told me that God had a special purpose for me. I tried to escape ministry. I earned degrees and gained experience working in business because I didn't want to do ministry. Like Jonah, my stubbornness is no surprise to God. I have no doubt that Jonah's experience brought an unsurpassable passion to his ministry in Nineveh. I've never spent time in the belly of a fish, but my experience has changed me. I'm sure Jonah looked and felt differently after he was vomited out. My experience, although not as exciting, influences my ministry in the same way. I, like Jonah, bear the scars of my experience. My experience allows me to see Christianity through a different lens. Just as a business is about profit, God is solely focused on you. You are his prize and his profit. And just as an army wages war to defend its country, God fights on your behalf daily. I wrote this book to help show you are important you are to him.

I will continue to share my experiences throughout the book. I share my experiences to illustrate that there is nothing extraordinary about me. I am not deserving to do ministry on any level. My experiences should illustrate that God can use anyone for his work. If I can be used, then God can use you. In the next chapter we will discuss the mission, or the direction, in which God uses us.

Chapter Two
When the Salt Has Lost its Flavor

Have you ever asked yourself, "What is the point of church?" "Is this God stuff even real?" "How is it supposed to affect my life?" I know I have. Throughout my life, I've had times where I have questioned my existence and my importance to God. I've questioned if going to church really makes a difference in my life and in the lives of others. I was born into a Christian family. As a child, I learned all the Bible stories and the exhaustive list of Christian don'ts. As a pastor's son, I mastered the art of disguise. I portrayed one image at church and a different image outside of the church. But as an adult, I've had to change the tune of my song. I've had to come to grips with the idea that what I was taught might not be what is necessarily best. I had to discover for myself the true reason for the church's existence.

The Bible describes the purpose of the Christian church. Jesus himself commanded his disciples to go throughout the world and to do his work. He promised to be with them until the end as they taught and baptized the world.[3] The later writings seem to expound on this purpose of the church body. It went beyond teaching. The purpose of church and those who make up the institution is to grow

---

[3] Matthew 28:19

together, to encourage one another,[4] and to love one another.[5] As Christians, we should pray together[6] and eat together[7] because we are family. Christians are to show the world God's love and grace[8] as a united community. This is the original mission of the church: to be together in unity while witnessing to the world what you have experienced. Jesus even said, "By this shall all men know that you are my disciples, if you have love for one another."[9] The church is a community. Simply put, the mission of the church should be to love and to attract others to Jesus with love. Jesus made one statement that describes Christianity, "Follow me and I will make you fishers of men."[10] That is the test of Christianity. The purpose of following Jesus is ministry. Jesus said, "You are the salt of the earth. But what good is the salt if it has lost its flavor? Can you make it salty again? It will be thrown out and trampled underfoot as worthless."[11] But what happens when we stray away from ministry or ministry doesn't work?

I am of Caribbean heritage, and we enjoy our food with seasoning. There are times when I taste food and my hand will instinctively reach for the salt. I know that salt will enhance the flavor of my food and make it palatable. Just as I look to salt to enhance the flavor of my food, Jesus views us, his followers, as seasoning. Our purpose is to be impactful and change the flavor of the world. This is Jesus' message. Jesus had a way of portraying this message through stories and analogies called parables. Jesus inserted his message into the people's experience and enhanced their lives in a way that was practical.

---

4   1Thessalonians 5:11

5   1 John 3:11

6   Philippians 4:6-7

7   Acts 2:42

8   Acts1:8

9   John 13:35

10   Matthew 4:19 KJV

11   Matthew 5:13 NLT

The Parable of the Talent

One day I was reading to my daughters, Abigail and Grace. We have a routine to read before they go to bed for the evening. This particular time, they chose a book that my wife, Salina, had bought from the dollar store. The story was Jesus' parable of the talents. Although I had heard the story numerous times, that day it changed my outlook on Christianity.

One day the master was preparing to go away to a far land, but before he left, he gathered his servants together. He told them about his trip, but while he was away, he still wanted to see his money working. So, he divided up his money between his servants according to the servant's abilities. To one he gave five coins; he held this servant in high regard. To another he gave two, and to another one. The servants with multiple coins invested, worked, and hustled while the master was away. But the servant with a single coin dug a hole, put the coin in it for safekeeping, and rested.

When the master arrived back home, he commended the servants with the multiple coins when he learned of their performance. They had both worked hard and doubled their master's investment in them. He was proud of them.

The third worker had buried his coin, and upon the master's return, he dug it up. The master was furious; it was the ultimate disrespect. He had been away on a long journey and the servant had not been productive with his time or his money. The servant demonstrated that he did not understand the master or his priorities.[12]

To me this story is a perfect allegory of our situation right now. Our master has gone on a long trip to prepare a place for us.[13] We expect him to return soon. Our master has given us a message, and told us

---

[12] Matthew 25: 15-30
[13] John 14:2,3

9

to go out and fish for people, but often our message is buried inside of our churches. Do we understand our master and his priorities? Will we choose to be faithful workers, or bury our talents and squander time?

I view the scriptures as a series of allegories to help our current situation. Every allegory, especially the parable of the talents, tells me that we need a change in the way we do church. Are we, as followers of Jesus, faithful in our ministry? Are we truly being fishers of people? I cannot speak for the church, but I can speak for myself. I know I don't use all of the talents that God has given me. The fear of failure, pain of rejection, and a host of other excuses prevent me from utilizing all the talents that God gave me. I always try to put things off until later. Life has a way of reminding us that we are on borrowed time. I need to use my talents today. I'd like to encourage you to use yours also. Don't be shy! Fail and fail hard, because you will stand up stronger.

Organizational Parallels

Before Jesus was made flesh, several Old Testament prophets described his life, including Isaiah, Micah, Malachi, and Zechariah. However, God's people constructed their own image of the Messiah. When Jesus walked the streets of Israel, his people did not recognize him because of the image the people had constructed. People had coded their spirituality to become a set of computer language-like rules, if this, then that. Their religious infrastructure was divided into sects to face off over doctrine. When the son of God was crucified on the cross, it signified the end of that religious infrastructure. Today that same infrastructure has been reconstructed by Christianity. Each of the over 600 denominations, or divisions, has its own unique interpretation of the scripture, despite Paul's warning.[14] Jesus came to simplify our rules down to two: love God, and love your neighbor as

---

[14] 1 Corinthians 1:10

yourself.[15] In other words, be a community that loves God and people. In the parable of the good Samaritan,[16] the priest and the Levite, leaders in the church, failed to help the man in need, a member of their community. Today it is easy to do the same and turn our back and show the same apathy to suffering. At times, I've found myself passing those in need without a second thought. There is a lurking danger in this. We can develop apathy to suffering. It is very easy for suffering to become so normal to us that it no longer concerns us. Being apathetic to suffering is unlike Jesus.

Despite not being recognized, Jesus came with a revolutionary new ministry. He healed the sick, he fed the hungry, and he went to the homes of sinners. He taught his followers to do the same. Through his actions he connected service with God. In Matthew 25, Jesus went a step further by connecting service with himself. He said that when you do so unto the least of them you've done it unto me. It went a step further than helping people because they are children of God. He commanded us to help others because in doing so, we help him.[17] He instructed us to serve not only those within our communities, but to serve all. He demonstrated how to launch and execute a revolutionary ministry.

The ministry we do today needs to be just as revolutionary and must go far beyond the walls of the church. People have needs, and each one of those needs is an opportunity for us to share Jesus. I am sure that you have needs. If you are in a church family, does your church meet those needs? Do you assist in meeting the needs of others around you? Sometimes all we need is a listening ear or a warm hug. It may not always take a church organization to meet our needs or to meet the needs of a community. Church needs to be revolutionary

---

[15] Luke 10:27

[16] Luke 10:30-37

[17] Matthew 25:40

and dynamic if it is to meet people's needs. It should not be business as usual. I encourage you to quit doing normal church.

Jesus, The Revolutionary

When I think of a modern revolution I think of the iPhone. I remember going out to purchase my Sony Walkman so I could play my cassette tapes. I remember sitting on the bus trying to listen to my CD player without it skipping on every pothole. And then came the iPod. The iPod was a market disruption. There was nothing Sony could do to sell the Walkman or the bulky CD player after the iPod was introduced. This revolution continued with the different types of iPods and MP3 players and then came the iPhone. And the market disruption by Apple started again. Jesus' ministry technique created a market disruption in his community and in the world. He led the largest religious market disruption that the world has ever seen. Jesus was and is a revolutionary leader. Jesus disrupted ministry as usual in his community. And we should aspire to disrupt the world's standard of the status quo when it comes to being Christians and living a life of ministry. What if we could quit doing normal church?

The task of a leader is to achieve results through others. The true test of a great leader is what happens after their departure. Judging by these criteria, Jesus is the most phenomenal leader the world has ever seen. There are around 2.2 billion people on this planet today who claim to follow his revolutionary ways. Jesus attended the synagogue, the church of his time, as was the custom. But Jesus' ministry was not dependent on the church. He took ministry beyond the temple to the unchurched, the sick, the poor, and the sinners. Jesus ministered to those whom the church did not accept. He was a line -crosser and a barrier-breaker. The religious law was to stay away from lepers, not talk to women, and not touch the dead. The law implied that the sick should stay sick, the unclean remain unclean, and the dead should stay dead. But Jesus crossed all those lines. Every day he sought to bring glory to God. Unlike us, Jesus took no days off.

On one occasion Jesus fed over 5000 men, plus women and children.[18] This multitude of people had come to listen to Jesus. His disciples wanted to send the people away to find their own food. Jesus recognized this situation as an opportunity to teach his disciples and bring glory to God. Jesus multiplied the gift of a boy's lunch and instructed the disciples to divide the people into groups. He then provided the disciples with the food to provide to the people to feed themselves. Jesus empowered the disciples, who empowered the people to serve each other. This miracle to me is another allegory of how church should be. Jesus nurtured the disciples while he taught them to nurture others.

Jesus only sought to do the will of his father, seeking no accolades for himself, only glory for God. Even at his last meal with his team, Jesus exuded humility. He girded himself with a towel and washed the disciple's feet,[19] demonstrating to us how to nurture ministry with humility. Do our ministers exhibit the same humility today? With that same humility, we should be reaching out to those whom Christianity has pushed away. Not even to bring them back to the church, but to bring the church to them. When someone is missing from the church, a member of the team is missing. In the same way, you are missing from the Kingdom of God, and Jesus is searching for you.

Jesus' life was a demonstration of service, not of sermonizing. He tangibly showed his love to the world. What is the main product of Christianity today? Every weekend the world hears thousands of sermons. Do we sermonize more than we serve? Does our Christianity talk too much?

---

[18] Luke 9:10-17
[19] John 13:1-17

Service to Sermon Ratio

Jesus' main activity was service, and it was far more impactful than his sermonizing. Jesus' actions spoke far louder than his voice. His actions are what drew people to his words. On one occasion, John the Baptist's disciples came to Jesus and asked, "Are you the one or should we find another?"[20] He could have chosen to outline his doctrine for them or expound upon the kingdom of heaven. Instead, Jesus told them to go back and report to John what they had seen. The evidence of his divinity was the silky-smooth skin of the Samaritan leper.[21] The joyful laughter of the widow's son[22] and Jairus' daughter[23] spoke far louder than any man's voice ever could. The calm demeanor of the ex-demoniac bible worker[24]as he ministered to those around him spoke volumes. Jesus chose to let his actions speak. Yet every week there are at least 300,000 different sermons preached in churches in the United States alone.

John 3:16 says, "For God so loved the world that he gave his only begotten son."[25] Jesus demonstrates that God is not big on saying I love you. God shows his love through action, and Jesus did the same. Jesus showed his love to people through service. Action was his sermon of choice. To me service is how we know this whole Jesus thing is real. Seeing the impact following Jesus makes on people in our community and in our world is how we know it is real. Our Christianity should cure the world of its problems by aiming to serve the needs of people. Not just service to those we deem as "saved," but service to all.

---

[20] Matthew 11:3
[21] Luke 17: 12-18
[22] Luke 7:11-17
[23] Mark 5:21-43
[24] Mark 5:1-20
[25] John 3:16

Jesus Said "Go!"

In his last encounter with the disciples Jesus gave instructions. He said, "Go ye therefore and teach all nations, baptizing them in the name of the Father, and of the Son, and of the Holy Ghost."[26] God wants us to use what he has given us to work towards glorifying him while he is away from us physically. Jesus says that everyone who says "Lord, Lord" is not his friend.[27] He is looking for those who are about that action. What if we were to take his revolutionary example and serve others? What if we were to switch our sermons for actual service? Jesus describes his faithful servants in the Bible.[28] This description shows that we must convert words to actions.

Jesus expects for his followers to do just that in their communities throughout the world. Our mission is to go into the world and teach and baptize. We are to show love and enhance the flavors of the communities we are in; that is our mission. We are the salt that is to give flavor to the earth. Songs, sermons, and church programs are the tools we choose to achieve that mission, but these things alone cannot change a community. When Jesus said "Go!" his disciples founded Christianity. But somewhere along the line, Christians stopped being adaptive to change to meet the needs of society. Any organization that does not adapt to change dies. When we do not adapt our methods, we lose relevance, we lose influence, and we lose our flavor.

What do we do when the salt has lost its flavor? How do we know when the flavor is lost? The salt has lost its flavor when it fails to be an agent of change in the community. The salt has lost its flavor when we prioritize church programming over service to those in need. The salt has lost its flavor when the world no longer cares that we exist.

A problem with church today is that there is a large and growing

---

[26] Mathew 28:19

[27] Matthew 7: 21-23

[28] Matthew 25:35-40

population who do not connect with church on a basic level. There should be some kind of alternative community for people who could benefit from that community but may not want to go to a traditional church. We saw the ministry of Jesus and how his revolutionary ministry demonstrated love. That love extended beyond the walls of the temple. It is important for us as Christians to be flexible to our method, but consistent in our mission. Does our church demonstrate that same love to our changing world, or do we just talk about it? When the salt has lost its flavor, we can ask God for it back. But before we learn how to ask for it back, let's learn why he would give us back our flavor. Let me ask you this: how salty are you?

Your church may or may not help you to fulfill the purpose of church. Does your church change the "flavor" of your community? How can you use your talents to help you to grow spiritually? Often the church organization is too large to support the talents of the individual. Spiritual growth and the use of your talents is your responsibility. Please do not allow fear to stop you from using the talents that God gave you. I believe that your talents can take you and ministry beyond the walls of the church. Most of all, the aim of this chapter is to encourage you to quit doing normal church. Use your talents for God and prioritize service over sermons. Execute the church's mission to love, and attract others by your love. You have the power to do so. In the next chapter we'll talk about why.

Questions to Consider:

I encourage you to write down the answers to these questions. There is something powerful that occurs when our words are written down. It is the beginning of the process of converting your words into action.

- ✓ Do you see yourself in any of the Bible stories?
- ✓ How did Jesus demonstrate his love?
- ✓ What is your spiritual mission?
- ✓ What is the purpose of church for you?
- ✓ Is your church resistant to change?
- ✓ Are you resistant to change?
- ✓ Does your church prioritize sermons over service?
- ✓ How can you be about that action?
- ✓ How can you be a change in your community?

Chapter Three
The Divine Connection

I am a superhero. I don't usually wear my cape in public, but I am a superhero. My superpower is my connection with God. You have the same superpower also. Let's talk about it.

The Bible tells us that a friend can sometimes be as close to us as a blood sibling.[29] Have you ever had a friend so close that you don't have to say hello when you call? You and your friend are comfortable enough with each other to skip formalities. When you have to, you can call them and begin to unload or you can call them just to say "hello". No matter what, you know that friend is always there. It seemed like God and Isaiah had that type of relationship. I read my Bible with an active imagination. My imagination tells me a story about the way the book of Isaiah begins. I imagine God and Isaiah's friendship being close enough for them to skip formalities. God says, "Sons have I reared and brought up, but they have rebelled against me. The ox knows its owner, and the ass its master's crib; but Israel does not know, my people does not understand."[30] God was mad and because of their friendship, shared those feelings with Isaiah. The

---

[29] Proverbs 18:24
[30] Isaiah 1:2,3 RSV

Israelites, God's chosen people did not claim Yahweh as their God and that was the source of frustration. They acted like they did not know to whom they belonged as if they had no connection to him at all. God had made a promise to Abraham to make his children into a great nation. Now the promise had been fulfilled, but the people seemed to have forgotten what God had done for them.

Unfortunately, I believe this story relates to us today. We may not be able to trace our blood line to Abraham, but if we follow Jesus we are spiritually his descendants. God wants us to understand and take that connection seriously. We should want to keep our connection as strong as we can possibly make it. To perform our job as his children we must first understand the connection that we have with our creator. We must understand that connection to understand why God would do so much for us. This connection is the catalyst for action.

The gospel, like you and I, doesn't travel very far without a vehicle. I don't walk far to reach my destination because I know I am going to have to walk back and that's more work than I'd like to put in. If I want to go far, I jump in my car, my vehicle. Your experience is the vehicle for the gospel to travel to the far ends of the earth. When you boldly share your spiritual encounter and experiences with others with passion and enthusiasm, you become the vehicle for God's work to be done. Your connection with divinity will connect you with people, and the way you share your experience will make all the difference.

Jesus came to emphasize and strengthen the connection we have with God. The Bible says, "For we have not a high priest which cannot be touched with the feeling of our infirmities; but was in all points tempted like as we are, yet without sin."[31] Traditionally, the high priest is one that relates to the people yet is deeply connected

---

[31] Hebrews 4:15-16 KJV

with divinity. Jesus can be our high priest because he relates to our struggle, having walked in our shoes, and he also shows us his divinity through his performed miracles and infinite wisdom. Because I believe it is of the utmost importance, I'd like to highlight three ways that we connect with God. These three ways are not the only ways that we connect, but they relate to our mission to draw people to Jesus. The world is connected to God through us; therefore, I want to highlight ways in which we can do our good work and build the kingdom through sharing our connection with The Father.

Creative Connection

Creation does not happen by itself. This world did not come into existence because of the "big bang," though many may believe in that theory. The iPhone did not come into existence when a flip phone fell into a bucket of radioactive water. Just like the iPhone, this world was designed and created. Your mom was and still is right — that bed is not going to make itself. Before a creation can happen, there must first be an idea or a vision to create something. Solutions are created to solve problems and good solutions solve many problems. We are solutions to vindicate God's name from Lucifer's accusations. (We will talk about this more later.) This seems like a big role to have, right? We were created in the image of a God that is thought so highly of us that we were given dominion over the entire earth. This was the case until Adam and Eve met evil in the Garden of Eden.

The very first story we are told in the Bible is the basis for everything else we know about God. God created the heaven and earth, and then God created us.[32] Characteristics of God are written into our DNA. The creativity in our DNA is a reflection of God. The church itself should be a fountain of innovation and creativity

---

[32] Genesis 1

cultivation. When we allow church to be a place that cultivates that creativity, especially in our young people, we will find ministry to be highly effective.

The world's finest art gallery has nothing on the Grand Canyon. No creation of man can match the northern lights, or even the sunset outside your window. God's creativity is dense and diverse. It is amazing to think that the same God that made the Sahara Desert made the icebergs. The same God that made the Grand Canyon made Mt. Kilimanjaro. And the same God that made the stars in the sky made the Great Barrier Reef. The finest work that a person's hands can make would never have anything on God's creation. Each creative work that we do is a tiny reflection of the Almighty. Our creativity is one of the ways in which we connect with God. The reflection of God is so strong in us that people often mistake that reflection for a sign that they are God. We as human beings do not have the answers to all problems. And that's a good thing. But God does allow us to use the part of our being that reflects divinity to stir up creative concepts to make things happen for us and for those around us.

We are told that all things are possible through God's strength.[33] Because we ought to believe this to be true, there is no thinking outside the box, because for Christians, there is no box. "The box" is a symbol of limited thoughts, ideas, and resources. Because God is powerful and all knowing, we have access to an unlimited resource, no boundaries to our creativity. Having no box expands our capability for creativity. How can we use that creativity to connect others to God also?

I love dancing with my daughters. I almost cry every time because they dance as if nobody is looking. Their dancing is an expression of their happiness. Their dancing is so creative. They don't watch television, so there is very little imitating of things they've seen. I

---

[33] Philippians 4:13

see pure happiness coming out; it gets wild and I never want it to end. There is an innocence that dies in children as they grow older and a certain point where creativity is assassinated. Children start to believe the negative things people say. Their creativity is stifled by the ways of the world around them. Often, experiencing life makes children fearful of expressing creativity. Children instead learn to follow instructions and they learn to play by the rules set for them. By the time a child enters adulthood that inclination to change the world has died. Children's creativity and desire to change the world reflects the Creator. Adults must unlearn some things to unlock their creativity, but with children that is not necessary.

One morning at breakfast my, daughter Abigail asked me to draw her and her sister. I replied, "I can't draw. You are the artist of the family. You are very good; you draw you." She replied, "Yes you can daddy; you have hands!" I realized that my drawing is still at a four-year-old level, because that was probably the age that I began to believe I could not draw. In fact, I was created to be an artist; I have hands! But I chose not to cultivate that talent. I was born with a special potential to change my world, but at some point, I began to believe that I could not. Fortunately, young people are still crazy enough to believe that they have the creativity to change the world and do something special. That is why so many of our world's innovations come from younger generations. Please believe that you are special enough to change the world. Don't let anyone tell you that you cannot when Jesus said that you can.[34] God created you to be a creator. Your creativity connects you with your creator. When we create, we reflect God. That is why when we write things down, especially goals, something special happens. It is the beginning of that creative process that reflects God in us. Tapping into your creative gift allows God to create something marvelous in you.

---

[34] Matthew 19:26

The Tear Connection

Jesus came to illustrate his connection with us and our human problems. The Bible tells us that the Messiah would be a man of sorrow.[35] Jesus' friend Lazarus died; we are told that "Jesus wept."[36] Jesus came to show that no matter how unfortunate a situation, God can relate to it. The gospels acknowledge Jesus as a man of sorrow. He looked upon the people with pity, because they had no shepherds.[37] He was perplexed and sorrowed by the religious infrastructure at that time. We saw him in sorrow praying to his father and sweating drops of blood in the garden of Gethsemane.[38] Jesus was beaten and crucified for crimes he did not commit. He was mocked, abused and spat upon by the same people he came to save. Jesus was indeed a man of sorrow, He did not have a very happy life. Have you ever been through a situation that brought you to tears? The tears that flowed from your eyes are the same tears that flowed from the eyes of Jesus. Jesus came to connect with our tears. Tear shedding reveals opportunity. The pain that Jesus encountered transformed into glory for his Father. If we are followers of Christ we would follow him in converting pain into glory for God. For a Christian, every tear is an opportunity to give God the glory and to connect people to Christ.

It was the summer of 2012. I had just graduated from Alabama State University in Montgomery, Alabama. I was awaiting my orders to begin military service as a project officer at Hanscom AFB in Massachusetts. As I melted in the Montgomery heat, my phone rang; it was my Aunt Kathy. She advised me to go and see my father, in England. She revealed that he had pancreatic cancer. I told her I would go when I saved some money. She insisted that I go immediately

---

[35] Isaiah 53:3

[36] John 11:35

[37] Matthew 9:36

[38] Luke 22:44

and even paid for my flight. I was elated that I was going home to see my dad.

Honestly, I didn't think anything of it all. My dad was a superhero. Nothing could beat him. Clearly my Aunt Kathy had forgotten who my dad was. The last time we spoke, he told me not to worry; he'd be fine. I'd never seen him sick, so it was easy to believe him. He was strong, fast, and smart. What I didn't know when we spoke was that my father had been bedridden for weeks. When I got home I saw the strong, broad, muscular frame of my dad had wasted away, but he got out of bed to greet me. We spent the summer together, taking walks, talking, and spending time together as a family laughing. My dad was a preacher and I remember many of his sermons, but this real-time sermon I was watching him preach, in battling cancer, is the sermon I will never forget. His friends visited him expecting to see a man dying. Instead, our home was filled with love and laughter on a daily basis. He visited the sick, spoke in church, and he got stronger every day. And from what I could see, he was recovering.

I received my military orders; I had to report for duty no later than September 30, 2012. I left home on September 12 to go and get my things from Alabama. Dad was gaining strength and I promised him I would be back to see him for his birthday in April. And as life would have it, before I made it to Boston, my Dad passed away.

His funeral was held on a cold Tuesday morning. Over 2000 people battled London traffic to pay respects. I later realized that God allowed my dad's situation to become a lesson for me. I was given the opportunity to watch and be a part of the life of a great man. And in this, I grew closer to Jesus than I had ever been. I'm not a crier. I never cry, but on that day, tears flowed freely. For me, those tears were a sign of my growth. Those tears were a way of relating to others. Those tears were an opportunity to understand myself. That day I had to admit to myself that I do cry sometimes, and it is okay.

Often God uses tragedies to wake us. God, in his ultimate wisdom, knew that today's world would be crazy. God knew there would be no shortage of tears, pain, or suffering. Diseases, violence, hatred, and injustice are ever increasing. God could have chosen to connect himself and his son with wealth and riches galore, but instead he chose to associate with suffering. As many in the world turn a blind eye, imagine what would happen if a few Christians saw tears as an opportunity to glorify God. Jesus was one person, and look at the difference that His actions made globally. You are a part of his movement. Tears and pain are a connection to God and every tear you shed brings you one step closer to your creator. Tears are unfortunate, but they are an opportunity. Don't miss the opportunity.

The Passionate Connection

Passion is the most sought-after commodity on earth. People spend much time and money seeking their passion and the passions of others. We watch television and are moved by the passion of the actors. We follow sports and cheer for the passion of the athletes. Yet there is nothing more passionate than when someone dies for what they love, hence the phrase, "to die for." We say things like, "This chocolate is to die for," but no one is going to die for some chocolate. Jesus says, "Greater love hath no man than this, that a man lay down his life for his friends."[39] Jesus gave up his life for his friends. He was willing to give up everything for his friends. He laid aside heaven and divinity, to come down to the hood of Nazareth to die for us, his friends.

It seems like since Jesus' era, the hood has continued to produce extraordinary people. The people of Jesus' time would say, "What good can come from Nazareth[40]?" Around the time Jesus was born,

---

[39] John 15:13
[40] John 1:46

before he moved to Nazareth of the Galilee region, there was a rebellion. Nazareth and that region were the home of many zealots, men who were against the Roman occupation. They staged a revolt against the Roman nation. As a response to the revolt, the Roman army came down upon the region. They killed the men. The women were raped, and they destroyed everything. Jesus lived in Nazareth in the aftermath of this destruction by the hands of the Romans. This tragedy made the men of the region yearn for the coming of the Messiah. Nazareth was not just a poor neighborhood; it was a neighborhood that had been ravaged. There was nothing fruitful there.

To me, it seems like poverty can be a breeding ground for passion, and sometimes success. Look how many celebrities came from Nazareth-like situations. Jim Carrey, Tom Cruise, Jenifer Lopez, to name a few. Look at the children of the former slaves who came to the United States in the bowels of ships. Passion can be bred from unfortunate situations.

The story of landfill harmonics illustrates how passion can be bred from poverty. In Cateura, Paraguay, 2,500 families live in an area that is prone to flooding. Cateura is a landfill. The children collect the trash and resell it. Illiteracy is rampant and when it rains, the town floods with polluted water. A violin is worth more than the homes so the inhabitants cannot afford to play instruments. Once, a music teacher moved to Cateura because wanted to add music to the lives of the residents. He found a way to make instruments from the trash found in the landfill. Some of the instruments made were violins, cellos, basses, guitars and drums. The teacher formed an orchestra with the neighborhood children. Their passion was channeled through their music. The poverty-stricken children from Paraguay began to tour around the world with their trash can instruments. Their passion caused them to outgrow their situation.

Passion is often discovered from a place of pain. This is evident in the story of the children from Cateura. This is also evident when you look at the backgrounds of many that are considered as successful. Much of the success we see in the United Stated comes from the children of the stolen — the slaves. Is this because of the pain that was inflicted on their ancestors? This same passion is evident, to me, in the story of Jonah. I ask myself, would the Ninevites have been convicted to repent if Jonah had not had his belly-of-a-fish experience? Was Jonah's success in convincing the Ninevites to repent due to the pain he experienced? If this theory is true, we have good news. The good news is that pain does not come without promise. From our pain, passion can be drawn, and that passion is what the world needs. When our passion is combined with our God-given talents, amazing things happen.

There is nothing that can match the intensity of a passion that comes from pain. What you are passionate about may be what God created you to do. It is your way of connecting people to him. It is our duty as his friends and followers to take what we are passionate about and use it to share his love. The Bible tells us that we will overcome by the blood of the Lamb and by the word of our testimony.[41] Tears, creativity, and passion for God will fill our testimonies. Our testimonies are the vehicles that will move the gospel. Our testimony is a vehicle for us to overcome our struggles when we use them to empower others. What experiences have created a passion in you?

I believe life is about learning how to convert our pain into passion and our passion into praise. This is a difficult lesson to learn, but it is invaluable once learned. I have learned that you have to be careful what you ask God for. I asked God to increase my faith, and this is the lesson I was taught. When I ask God for something, I usually receive it in ways that I had not imagined. I asked God for

---

[41] Revelation 12:11

patience, I got a wife and two daughters. Patience takes a long time to develop, but the three ladies in my life are helping it to develop.

The lesson in trust has been a difficult one. I talk about our experience moving to California in the next chapter as I share how prayer can be a solution. A year after that breakthrough, I found myself in the same situation, without a job. I learned that God has continually been there for me. I learned to remember what God has done for me in the past and not to worry. I learned not to spend time worrying and to seek the good even from bad situations. If we can learn to find the good even from bad situations we can become invincible. Life sends us a multitude of situations that may test us and break us down, if we can find good in them. As this book is being finalized, I have no job, but I am not unemployed; I am free. I am in God's hands. I'm learning to trust in God's plan for me. I've learned to not ask God for anything, I can't take too many lessons. I've learned to just say thank you instead. But I am grateful because of the opportunity in pain.

Multiple times in the Bible it talks about growth. We admire the bodies of people who have worked out. We wish our bodies could be the same way. We see the end state but we do not see the work, sweat, and sometimes tears that it took to get them that way. The opportunity in pain is from the resistance. Resistance to our plans often results in tears. Bodybuilders illustrate that resistance can be used to shape us, and define us. I choose to believe that through my tears, through my pain, and through my creativity God is shaping me. That is the opportunity in pain.

Getting the Church Involved

On June 14, 2017, a fire raged in North West London. Grenfell Tower, a 24-story residential building, was ablaze. The first call for the fire came after midnight, when people were asleep in their beds. The fire was unquenched for about 60 hours. People trapped inside the building could be seen screaming for help by their concerned neighbors and friends. The building was home to 600 people, 80 of whom were confirmed dead, and 70 wounded. This tragedy impacted all London residents. It forced them to come together, as tragedy often does.

Churches sprang into action, facilitating help for the victims by becoming donation centers. Churches became hubs from which help was deployed. The church used their creativity; their choirs and musicians held fundraising concerts. They used their tears and empathized with the victims, providing them with emotional and spiritual help. This tragedy invoked a passionate response that united Londoners. The response to this tragedy was nothing short of awesome. This was an example of Christians being faithful.

My question is must tragedy strike for us to see mobilization like this? How can our organizations be set up to exhibit community involvement on a regular basis? Not behaving as a mass body, as if there is a constant tragedy needing attending to, causes the church to lose its flavor. It is in action that we keep our connection with God and we continue to salt the earth as the church. How can we stay in action?

You are God's solution, and he does not leave you alone. You are connected to the most powerful being in the universe. The creator of the world knows your name. In fact, that creator DNA runs through your veins. Jesus came to enhance and illustrate that connection for us. Every tear that we shed connects us with Jesus. Let's use that connection to grow our passion and to grow spiritually. Your passion is exactly what the world needs. Remember that you are a superhero. We've discussed our mission and our connection. What is the next step in this process to be faithful? The precursor to all effective Christian action is prayer. It is prayer than helps to guide our efforts.

Questions to Consider:

- ✓ How do you express your creativity?
- ✓ What experiences have created a passion in you?
- ✓ What are you passionate about?
- ✓ What tears have you shed that connect you with others?
- ✓ How can you combine your passion and your creativity?
- ✓ What community need does your passion connect with?
- ✓ How can you use your creativity and your passion to glorify God?
- ✓ What does being faithful look like to you?
- ✓ Are you faithful? If not, how can you be?

Chapter Four
Make Prayer a First Solution

We have a powerful tool, but it sits on our shelves as decoration as we suffer. Prayer, if used efficiently, would alleviate so much suffering and pain.

I would be remiss if I did not speak as honestly as I know how when it comes to the church and prayer. I believe that prayer has been deeply misrepresented. Prayer, at least to me, sometimes seems like it has become synonymous with doing nothing. Maybe this comes from living in the wake of so much tragedy, where people send their thoughts and prayers to situations even when something else is needed. Prayer sometimes seems like a pointless activity, performed when Christians cannot or will not do anything about a situation. It is my strong conviction that prayer is activity of power, and I'd like to share why.

The first step to any solution is to acknowledge that there is a problem. We must admit to God that there is a problem and that we know there is a divine solution. Prayer is always the best solution and it is our direct line to reach God. However, it is not always recognized as a solution. Sometimes prayer is seen as an excuse for inaction. People say, "Those Christians are just praying again!" Prayer should always lead to something. Sometimes it may lead to action; other times it might lead to inaction. Prayer should align us to God's will.

When we find there is nothing we can do, prayer becomes our only solution. In situations where we have no other option but to pray, we are most powerful. The awesome thing about God is that he created us with the power of choice. That's love, the power of choice. We can choose to deny God's existence, end even that does not affect God's love. Each time God blesses us we have the choice to either acknowledge the divine hand, or we can say, "Phew, that was lucky." In my personal experience, I have found prayer to be powerful solution and I acknowledge God's hand.

One of my pet peeves is when people tell me how to do a job I know how to do, especially when that person lacks the expertise in the area in which they are attempting to advise me. "Stay in your lane" is a phrase that falls from my lips quite often, along with "Let me do my job and you do your job." I examined the way I prayed and found that in my prayers, I would do the same thing to God. I would approach God with a grocery list of concerns. I'd proceed to tell God exactly how I expected to see those concerns resolved. I would boldly express thanks for response to my request, because I knew I could expect a resolution. But one day for some reason, I imagined that I was God listening to my prayer. I realized that if I was God, I wouldn't answer my prayer. It was as if God said to me, "Stay in your lane. Let me be God and you be Daniel."

I realized that God knows how to be God and doesn't need my prayer as advice. God's plans are better than mine. My biggest blessing is that I didn't receive all the things I prayed for. God's plan for me is far better than the plan I had for myself. I had to adjust the way that I pray and present myself before God. When things didn't go my way, I would interpret it as God not answering my prayer and thus didn't love me. Out of love for me God did not give me what I asked for. Imagine that you had a son whom you loved. You would not give him a new Porsche convertible in high school. He is not mentally ready for that power. Not giving us things simply because we asked for it does not imply poor divine parenting. I remember I asked God not to let my dad die when he was battling terminal cancer. Death, especially for someone suffering from a terminal illness, can be a release from pain. I would have been content seeing my dad in pain just so I could have him with me. I am thankful that God is much more merciful than I am. I learned to ask God not for what I want, but for what he wants for me. I changed the purpose of my prayers. Instead of listing requests, my prayers now declare my love for God and request help in trusting his divine plan.

A Plausible Solution

It is only when our request aligns with God's will for us that we see our prayers answered. Jesus showed us to pray for God's will to be executed on earth, just as it is in heaven.[42] As Christians, we should be agents of that action. We must pray for God's will to supersede our will. When we tell God that we trust the divine plans, our prayer then becomes a solution. When I decided to change the way I prayed, it seemed like that's when trouble came out of nowhere. All of a sudden, life became very uncomfortable for me. Unfortunately, growth mostly occurs when we are uncomfortable. If you are uncomfortable and going through a difficult time, smile. God is working on you, for you. Get ready to meet a new and improved you.

The year was 2013 and I was doing well as a young professional. My dream job in college was to be an officer in the United States Air Force and there I was, a Second Lieutenant. I was a project manager at Hanscom AFB in Massachusetts. Our mission revolved around supporting the warfighter and putting "warheads on foreheads." I was paid more than I had ever been, I had exciting projects, and I could support my new family. I should have been happy. But for some

---

[42] Matthew 6:10

reason, I became uncomfortable at my job. It just did not feel like I was fulfilling my real purpose, so I began to pray about it. After praying about it for some time, I encountered a few situations. I felt God revealed my calling to minister to troops as a chaplain. The plan for me to attend seminary began to unfold. I applied for the same school my dad attended, Andrews University in Michigan. But after several months of not getting a response to my application, I began to pray for an alternative solution. I discovered a similar program at La Sierra University in California, and even though I didn't want to go there, I applied. I applied because I felt moved to do so, but my heart was still set on attending Andrews. That was the first time I remember praying and asking for God's will and being willing to follow divine direction. I told God I would go wherever I was accepted first. Even in that prayer, I felt like I had the upper hand because I had applied for Andrews six months before I applied for La Sierra.

One Monday out of the blue, I received an acceptance letter from La Sierra University. The very next day I received acceptance letter from Andrews University. To be honest, I was thrilled about being accepted to Andrews, but I knew I had to be obedient. Preparations began for the big move to California, but everything was uncertain. I had no job prospects, no place for my wife and daughters to live, and no relatives nearby. The fact that my wife agreed to move could only be God.

Fast forward about three years and we were in California. I started school, but my family of four was living in a small two-bedroom apartment. The only job I could find was in Los Angeles and took over three hours each way to commute. My wife was not happy, and exhaustion had turned me into a zombie. One day, my wife stood in front of me crying. "Things are not working out here. I'm going back to Boston, whether you come with me or not." I thought back in my mind to that first time that I remember God leading me to change careers. I recalled the feeling that God was moving to get us to California. I thought back to the countless miracles that it took to get me to that position. God had worked everything out for us. I replied, "It wasn't my decision to come here. God called us out here, so I can't go back." All I could do was pray. There was absolutely nothing more I could do. Prayer was my only solution. I placed it all in God's hands — my career, my family, and most of all, my faith.

Seven days after I got up from my knees, my school called and offered us a three-bedroom house at my university. I received a job offer near our home, paying more than I had made before. We found a daycare for the girls around the corner from the new house. Around a month after that miracle, my wife was offered a position with the same organization I worked for. Who said real prayer did not work?

In my situation, prayer was my only solution. I'm sure you've had your own difficult situation for which prayer was your only option. When prayer is your solution, it gives you a different kind of humility. Knowing that there was nothing to to but allow God to be God. Someone may ask, what is the point of praying if God is going to do it for you anyway? The answer to that is simple: Because life is a growth experience, one must learn to trust God. One lesson that must be learned is that we are on a spiritual journey here on earth. And every part of the journey requires a different level of faith and action. When we pray in faith, we must take some kind of action that allows God to move and work in us and around us. The more God continues to bless me, I am constantly reminded of the times where desperation seemed to overtake me. I remember times like when I didn't have the gas money to get from Boston to California and the gifts of friends made the trip possible. God doesn't come on demand, but in God's own perfect timing. And his time is always on time. This Christian experience doesn't promise comfort, but it does promise growth.

God is not a genie. Just because we ask God for something, doesn't mean that we'll get it or that we deserve to get it. Times of struggle, although sometimes painful, are good for us to endure. At times our struggles are God's plan for us. Just because you struggle doesn't mean God has left you alone. Struggle, or adversity, is a matchmaker. Adverse situations introduce us to who we really are. And when our struggles continue, we must reach out to God to ask for the divine plan to be revealed to us. God can guide us as we discover ourselves and discover our mission.

Prayer is exactly what you need to understand your mission and passion so that you can use them to God's honor and glory. Don't quit when you don't get everything right the first time. God didn't trick you. God is testing you to prepare you for greater things. Listening to and following God sometimes looks foolish to those who don't have that kind of connection. But keep on anyway. Do not allow the opinions of others to cause you to doubt God. Guess what? You can pray about that too. God wants to know your concerns and wants to guide you to your next assignment in life. Prayer is far more than a solution. You will also find that prayer is a connection to the power that comes from God. But when do we need that connection, and how can we access it?

Prayer as a Connection

The ultimate goal of prayer is connection. Jesus taught us that prayer is a way of connecting with our Father in Heaven. Jesus came to show the effectiveness of prayer as a connection and as the solution. He taught his disciples how to pray,[43] but he also demonstrated to them its effectiveness. On multiple occasions, they saw the results of prayer. When Jesus first met Nathanael, he told him he saw him under the fig tree and Nathanael believed in him. Jesus replied, "You believe because I told you that? You will see way better things than that. You

---

[43] Matthew 6:9-11

will see the angels of God ascending and descending upon the Son of Man."[44] Jesus was referring to the connection opened by prayer.

My favorite example of this is the instance where Jesus fed the crowd of 5000. Jesus recognized the problem: the people needed physical and spiritual food. The disciples looked for a way to feed the people. They came back and said it would take more than a month's pay to buy food for all these people.[45] Jesus recognized this as an opportunity to demonstrate prayer as a solution. Prayer can only be a solution when you have the connection. Jesus blessed the few pieces of food they had, fed the multitudes, and had food left over. Jesus had the connection he needed to transform a dim situation into a beacon of hope and light.

Why should we pray? We should pray because we need to be constantly connected with the Father. Prayer acknowledges that things are out of your control and that you need a higher power to come through for you. It allows you to submit to that higher power in word and in action. Studies have shown that prayer is good for your health.

Prayer as a Stress Reliever

Stress is a killer. Stress depletes our immune system. When our immune system is down, our bodies are prone to attack from diseases. Johns Hopkins University recognizes that unresolved conflict is linked with poor health. The act of forgiveness is linked with good health. They encourage making forgiveness a part of your life and forgiving others as well as yourself.[46] Immediately following the Lord's Prayer, Jesus says to his disciples, "For if ye forgive men their trespasses, your heavenly Father will also forgive you: But if ye forgive not men their trespasses,

---

[44] John 1:48-51

[45] John 6:7

[46] http://www.hopkinsmedicine.org/health/healthy_aging/healthy_connections/forgiveness-your-health-depends-on-it

neither will your Father forgive your trespasses."[47] It seems like this rule was written into our very DNA, and Jesus knew that. Prayer is the first step towards forgiving someone and being loving. It is also a step towards living a life of freedom.

Our friends Josh and Jessica, our old neighbors/prayer partners, refer to arguments as intense moments of fellowship. If you are married you may find yourself intensely fellowshipping with your spouse. When I find myself in these intense moments with my wife, the solution is always to pray. I cannot be frustrated with someone after I have prayed. For me, prayer is always the beginning to forgiving my wife, or realizing I was wrong — mostly realizing I was wrong. In the same vein of fellowship, my daughters are two fireballs of energy racing at full speed towards each other. There are times that I cannot take it, especially in the middle of the night. I am tempted to snap at them in anger, which sometimes I do. I am learning to pray with them because I cannot be angry and pray at the same time. The two do not go together. Most of the time when I pray I get a feeling of peace and it relieves stress. Even at times when I don't feel that prayer alleviates my struggle, I feel more peace. I can feel peace because prayer has brought me closer to God. I have nothing to worry about when I am having a conversation with the Creator of everything. The feeling you get when you pray is what you need when starting this journey to become church. There is relief in acknowledging that everything is not dependent upon you and you are dependent upon God. Prayer declares that you are willing to follow God's plan.

The Journey

Prayer acknowledges that there is something bigger than you. Prayer allows you to surrender concerns to God. Jesus says, "When he, the

---

[47] Matthew 6:14-15 KJV

Spirit of truth is come, he will guide you into all truth: for he shall not speak of himself; but whatsoever he shall hear that shall he speak: and he will shew you things to come."[48] The Holy Spirit as a guide is like a sports coach. A sports coach guides his team through confrontations with another team. Through training, the coach empowers them for the victory. Hence, the growth experience. When the disciples received the Holy Spirit, the result was action and empowerment for themselves and for others.

In addition to the gift of peace, humility is a gift after you pray. Knowing that something amazing is about to happen and it does not come from you is a sure way to get humble quickly. My friends Tochi and Charlotte refer to this as Godfidence, a deep and great confidence in God. In becoming church, Godfidence is exactly what you need. Paul encourages Timothy by reminding him that fear does not come from God but power, love and a good judgment does.[49] That's Godfidence, and it is one of our greatest weapons as a believer.

The first step to any solution is to acknowledge the problem. The next step for a Christian is to take that problem and give it to God. This is easy to say, while worrying inside. But, knowing the power of prayer, what it connects you with, and its true potential will hopefully change the way you feel as well as the way you pray. Hopefully knowing the way that others may view prayer will also change the way you pray also. It has definitely changed the way I pray. I am intentional about making sure I pray when I tell someone else I am going to pray for them. I am intentional about ensuring that when I pray I listen to God. I am also careful about making sure I don't move on my own feelings, but I move on God's instruction. At times it is difficult to hear God, and other times it is very clear. The power of prayer needs to be shown and other people need to see

---

[48] John 16:13 KJV
[49] 2 Timothy 1:7

it. God doesn't bless me for me to keep it to myself. It's important to me to demonstrate that just because I'm praying doesn't mean I am not going to do anything. I believe the world needs to know that it's possible to pray standing up.

Before closing this chapter, I must issue a warning. Be careful what you pray for. I'm not saying don't pray, just think about it. God doesn't promise us comfort. Growing may not always seem fun. Throughout the process, keep praying. Throughout the process, keep praying. Do not abandon God because God will not abandon you.

My question to you before you take any action is, "Did you pray first?" Here are a few questions I believe would be beneficial in building your prayer life.

Questions to Consider:

✓ Have you seen the result of prayer in your life?
✓ Have you seen growth from struggle?
✓ Has adversity revealed your true character?
✓ How can you change the way you pray?
✓ How can you change your prayer from a routine to an action?
✓ How can prayer resolve your situation?
✓ How can prayer de stress you?
✓ How can prayer strengthen your connection?
✓ How can you focus on listening in prayer?

Chapter Five
Christianity as a Weapon

Often after people die their words are misconstrued. The ideals they stood for are forgotten. The principles that defined them are set aside. I think this definitely happened when Jesus died. Christianity is often synonymous with judgment. Many people are skeptical about stepping into a church for fear of being judged. It frustrates me that the man who said "Neither do I condemn you"[50] is portrayed to the world as judgmental. Jesus came to create a society that was free from judgment. He did not judge women, children, minorities, or sick people, so why do we? Jesus came to place us on the offensive against his adversary, to make us a weapon. But it seems like in our current setup, we are used as a weapon against each other. In this chapter I want to spend some time talking about you. You are amazing and God chose me to remind you of just how great you really are.

God's Perfect Creation

The design of our bodies are perfect. The ingenuity of their design is remarkable. The design is completely self-sustainable. Our bodies are

---

[50] John 8:11

designed to defend from attack, self-repair, and remove waste. They grow, learn, create, and reproduce. Hospitals are a recent invention. It is only in the last few centuries that diseases have increased to epidemic proportion. Our bodies are versatile. I find personal physical transformation amazing. A person can go from being skinny to stocky, or from 400lbs to 150lbs. People alter their own body composition beginning with their mind.

Human existence and condition is a beautiful, resilient, and self-motivating thing. You were created a real superhero. Humans weren't created with the ability to fly, to shoot webs from our wrists, or to have the super powers seen on television. We were created in the image of a creator. We have the potential to create things from our imagination. You are a masterpiece. Yes, I'm talking about you! Your body's potential for beauty, creativity, and love is infinite. But this beauty is no accident; God made this beauty for a purpose. To explain that purpose, I would like to invite you into my weird and wonderful mind. I invite you to be free to imagine with me. In my imagination, I am going to use Yahweh as the name of God. Yahweh is a form of the Hebrew name of God used in the bible.

Before there was anything, there was Yahweh. Yahweh created a perfect home called heaven and lived there. In this perfect home, Yahweh created amazing beings called angels. Some angels had many sets of wings, some could fly at great speeds, but all had beautiful voices. The environment in heaven was like a beautiful garden. There were huge trees, glass-like rivers and seas, but the center of everything was the throne. On the beautiful throne sat Yahweh, surrounded by an innumerable throng of angels. Each of these angels was losing their minds about how wonderful Yahweh is. They sang and shouted and flew around in circles.[51] Every so often they'd learn a new tidbit of information about Yahweh and they would remain in awe until

---

[51] Isaiah 6:1-3

they learned something new. They were always learning more and more about Yahweh. Can you imagine what this scene would be like in person?

Yahweh is the personification of love, and because Yahweh is love and love is choice, each creature had a choice. The angels loved, served, and worshipped Yahweh out of free will. The angel closest to the throne was a beautiful angel. His skin may have glistened like the characters in *Twilight*. I don't know exactly what it was, but something about him made him beautiful. This angel was more beautiful than the other angels.[52] This angel's name was Lucifer. Lucifer's beauty however, was nothing compared to the beauty of Yahweh.

One day Lucifer was away from the throne of Yahweh, at home. He was taking selfies and posting them on.... whatever they posted selfies on in heaven back then. He decided, "One day, I'm going to be like that; I'm going to be like the Most High.[53] He said out loud to himself, "I deserve praise, like Yahweh". He nodded to himself. His feelings continued to fester and grow until one day he decided to do something about it. He called an angel he knew out of earshot of anyone else and began to share his feelings with him. He leaned in towards the angel and whispered, "Yahweh isn't fair." Lucifer continued, "If I was in charge, sometimes we would praise you because you're pretty awesome." The other angel thought about it a little and nodded, "Yeah, you are right." "Let's take a selfie together," Lucifer suggested. They learned in and took the picture. Lucifer began to tell his story to any being that had ears.[54]

Yahweh, being all knowing, knew about Lucifer's dissatisfaction, and the rumors he was spreading, so Yahweh's son, Michael, was sent to talk to him. Michael approached Lucifer and said, "How's it going brother, can we talk for a minute.?" "For sure," Lucifer replied, anxious

---

[52] Ezekiel 28:13-14

[53] Isaiah 14:11-14

[54] Ezekiel 28:16

for the opportunity to sell his story to Yahweh's favorite angel. If he could convince Michael, his work would be accomplished. Michael motioned for Lucifer to sit down beneath a large beautiful tree. Twelve different fruit hung from the majestic branches. They looked like shiny Christmas tree ornaments. "So," Michael began, "I hear you have issues with the way things are. Let's talk about your concerns to see if we can make you happy again," says Michael. Lucifer jumped at this opportunity. "Michael, you are the most beautiful of all the angels. You sing so well. Why don't we ever stop to acknowledge how beautiful you are? Are you satisfied living in a heaven where Yahweh takes all the glory?" Lucifer continued, "If I were in charge, we would praise and worship you sometimes." "Let's take a selfie for your beauty," Lucifer suggested. "Lucifer," said Michael, completely ignoring his suggestion. "Yahweh is the creator and designer of everything, the giver of life, and Yahweh loves you. To acknowledge your own beauty is to acknowledge perfect handiwork." Lucifer sat in awe and silence and Michael got up to walk away. "Lucifer, I want us to talk again tomorrow. We want you to be happy." And Michael disappeared.

Lucifer sat for a while longer, then flew as high as he could so he could get a chance to think. Lucifer thought, "Yahweh did create everything; without Yahweh there would be nothing." But as he was flying over a shiny sea, Lucifer caught his reflection. He stopped to look at himself, and shouted at the top of his lungs, "Anybody who looks this good has got to be God!" He realized right at that point that he couldn't wait any longer. He couldn't risk another conversation with Michael. Truth, facts, and common sense were going to crush his dream of being God. Facts and truth were his enemy. In his mind, he decided that if he were going to do this, it had to be now. Lucifer began to fly faster than the speed of light towards the throne room of Yahweh. His mind was telling him to stop, but his body was telling him he needed praise to go with all his beauty.

BANG! Lucifer flung open the giant golden throne room door, and it resounded against the marble wall. The throne room went silent; all eyes were on Lucifer because nobody had ever heard a sound like that. It was the sound of anger, jealousy and malice; it was the sound of the beginning of a confrontation. Despite the commotion, love was still written all over the face of Yahweh. Lucifer's face screamed with envy. As Lucifer made his way towards the throne of Yahweh, Michael stepped forward. Calmly and gently he said, "Lucifer if you still have issues we can talk about them. Would you like to step outside with me and talk?" But talking to Michael was the last thing he wanted to do. The words of Michael would convince him to do what was right, and that was not necessarily what he wanted in this case. Thousands of sets of eyes watched the drama that was unfolding. Lucifer continued to walk, ignoring Michael's suggestion. As he walked, the anger transformed Lucifer from a beautiful angel to a ferocious dragon. Lucifer stopped and lifted his hand and pointed it past Michael to Yahweh accusingly. The angels gasped, and you could have heard a pin drop, if they have pins in heaven. "Your laws," Lucifer screamed at the top of his lungs, making the room rumble "are not fair, and you do NOT love us!" The accusations pierced the peaceful atmosphere of heaven. Some angels sided with Lucifer. The situation escalated because of the rumors Lucifer had been spreading. His tales divided the population of heaven; a third of heaven's population sided with Lucifer. And there was war in heaven, Michael and his angels fought against the dragon and his angels.[55] My imagination draws a blank on how angels or spirits would fight. Do they use light sabers? Yahweh ended up casting Lucifer and his angels into darkness, out of heaven.

A buzz replaced the tranquility of heaven. There was much mumbling amongst the angels who were faithful to God. "What if Lucifer was right?" the angels wondered. Yahweh's love and fairness was on trial in the universe. Michael and Yahweh surveyed the troubled

---

[55] Revelation 12:7

atmosphere of heaven together. As they scanned the horizon, their eyes met for a moment. In that wonderful moment, the most intricate and awesome plan ever made was born, and tears filled their eyes.

Yahweh would give Lucifer an opportunity to prove himself. Lucifer claimed that if he was God, things would be far greater. Lucifer claimed that he would "make heaven great again." Yahweh, the ultimate judge was on trial, so another judge was needed. Yahweh would have to summon his special weapons and the divine trial was set and Lucifer and his angels were banished to earth. There, Lucifer usurped the role as ruler. The third rock from the sun became a theater, staging the most gripping drama of the universe. The rest of the universe can see the results of Lucifer's rule.

Yahweh created humanity to be the judges in the divine trial.[56] The purpose of our human existence is to judge between the rule of Yahweh and the rule of Lucifer. In the end, we will judge angels and speak to the fairness of God's rule. We are humanity. We are to witness the pain, death, and cruelty of this world ruled by Lucifer. But we are more than just witnesses; we are God's agents bringing light to this dark world. Even if we have found ourselves to be participants in the sin, cruelty, and pettiness, it's not the end. Yahweh's plan includes a way to restore us that we may live in heaven. There's vacancy made just for us. But first, somebody had to be the sacrifice for us to get there.

Jesus' Suicide Mission

A suicide mission is a task so dangerous that the people involved are not expected to survive. The plan for our salvation is the most intricate and expensive plan ever implemented. The plan involved a suicide mission. The core of this plan was a sacrifice, and that was

---

[56] 1 Corinthians 6:3

the reason for the tears in the eyes of Yahweh and Michael. Michael, known to us as Jesus, had to go on a mission. On this mission, Jesus knew that he had to die. But because of Jesus' background knowledge of the situation, he knew that he was going into combat.

Lucifer is now known as Satan, which was Hebrew for adversary. At the time of Jesus' coming, Satan was attacking God's chosen people. They were under the rule of their Roman oppressors and a corrupt king, King Herod. Their religious structure imposed all types of laws and rules upon them. Meanwhile the poverty-stricken people were dying from sicknesses and diseases. In the middle of all this, Jesus was born in a barn in Bethlehem. Herod heard that a king was to be born in Bethlehem, so he sent his soldiers there to kill all newborns there. Joseph and Mary smuggled the baby Jesus to Africa[57] to escape the soldiers, and there he remained until he was a small boy. When King Herod died, Jesus returned to Israel and lived in a town called Nazareth.

Jesus began to counter the attacks of Lucifer. Jesus began to heal the sick, cast out the demons from people, and bring the dead back to life, and he gave all credit to his Father in heaven. He converted the people's pain into praise. He would visit the homes of the poor and ostracized to tell them about the kingdom of heaven. In a time where the temple was the place for ministry, Jesus was revolutionary. Jesus took his ministry beyond the walls of the temple. He quit doing normal temple ministry. He was renowned in Israel and people would flock to see him. He even took his ministry to the Samaritans, the known enemies of Israel. Jesus' mission was to convert the attacks of Lucifer into glory for God. Wherever Jesus went, people praised God. But Jesus went a step further; he taught others to heal and serve.[58] Jesus was on the offensive and was destroying the hold that Lucifer

---

[57] Matthew 2:14
[58] Matthew 10:1

had over the people. Jesus gave the people hope and taught others how to give hope. Lucifer saw all that was going on. He saw that he was losing, and he decided, "Jesus has to go!" Lucifer influenced the religious leaders to kill Jesus. On one sinful Friday, Jesus was tried, tortured, and crucified. But Lucifer's anger had gotten the better of him. Only those who had sinned were under his jurisdiction. Lucifer had no right to kill the Son of God, who had never sinned. In this act, Lucifer had gone too far, and the universe could see through his façade. The universe could see that God is love because he sent his child to atone for the sins of the world. Lucifer lost.

In all of this, God allowed us to still be alive and well. We are still here because God wants to give you and me an opportunity to choose to be on the winning side to return to heaven. God could have returned and ended things a long time ago, but he didn't. God is waiting for you.[59] Now you have your opportunity to be on the offensive as Jesus showed us to. To be a Christian is to be a weapon — a weapon that converts pain into praise.

The Ultimate Weapon

Jesus came to earth as a weapon against the adversary. His practice was to convert the attacks of Lucifer into glory for God. To be a Christian means to follow the example of Jesus Christ. If Jesus was a weapon, then what are we supposed to be? Is Satan offended and threatened by Christianity? Christianity is almost imprisoned in the weekends, a few hours on a Sunday or Saturday. In our worship time, we are concerned with what to eat and what to wear, both things that Jesus said don't worry about.[60] We might be more inclined to be a weapon if we paid attention to the words of Jesus.

---

[59] 2 Peter 3:13
[60] Matthew 6:25-34

Despite all of this, Christianity is still a weapon. You are a weapon. Christianity today has become a weapon turned backwards. Christianity is not always used as an outreach to those ostracized by society or crippled by the rampant injustice, but to attack them. We hear more of Christians who use their beliefs and actions to hurt others than to heal them. There are churches known for their hate speech against practically everybody. Do they represent Jesus? You are church, and you do not have to be judgmental. In fact, I encourage you not to be. It is difficult enough making right decisions for yourself. Why bog down your load by adding the decisions of others to your plate? When judgment against others is a part of our focus, we lose the ability to truly worship God with a pure heart and clean hands.

The weapon of Christianity is offensive to Satan and his kingdom. Christianity should be a solution to a struggling community, showing the love of God. Christianity should be converting any unpleasant situation into glory for God. But the truth of the matter is that your church may or may not be doing that. You may or may not be doing that. But Jesus didn't die for your church organization; he died for you. This book is about equipping you as an individual so you can then equip the church to do ministry effectively. This change starts with you. Whether you are a part of a church or not, you can be a weapon. I am confident that you can be the change necessary in your community because you live there and you see what's needed.

I live in Southern California. Every so often you see mountains that are glowing orange, and grey smoke will fill the sky. The vehement flames burn fierce and bright. Those glowing mountains are visible for miles. The spreading fire that turns the mountain to a beacon could be your church, or you. Passion is contagious, and results encourage other people. It only takes a spark to get a fire going. You could be that spark. You should be that spark. You do not have to be in a church to be that spark, to begin converting issues into glory for God. You can turn your passion into worship. Christianity is a journey of growth.

The ultimate growth is when you use your passion to ease the pain of people to bring glory to God. You could be that fire. Burn vehemently and passionately, and be a light to your world. Your passion will be contagious, and you will be offensive to God's enemy, Satan.

Weapon Preparation

God designed each of us for a purpose. He has given each of us something to be passionate about. That passion may be an indication to our purpose. Weapon preparation is aligning your passion with an issue that will bring God glory. Our Christianity must become customizable. When we customize our worship and make it practical, we can do it daily. When we can be practical and worship daily, we will see amazing growth. If you want to read a gripping account of God calling someone, I recommend you read *Set on Fire*[61] by Taurus Montgomery. Taurus is passionate about motivating people, especially young men. He has discovered that his passion is in motivating and ministering to student athletes. I know that passions are not discovered when you are in your comfort zone. Discovering passion is often uncomfortable. Have you discovered your passion? If so, how can you use it for God? If not, what can you do to discover it?

My passion is service. I would serve with my fraternity, my school, and serve with the Air Force. I used to promote parties, and I felt I enjoyed doing it. I think it was one activity I was best at, planning and hosting parties. I guess you could say it was my talent. I had to find a way to incorporate my talents and my passion into worship. I want to do that by combining my talent with my expertise in project management and creating solutions to connect people. I prepare my weapon by combining my passion and my talents into praise. Now I look at myself as a weapon in a divine conflict. There is one

---

[61] www.taurusmontgomery.com

situation that I look back on that has changed the way I look at my Christianity.

I was about 16 years old and I lived in London, England. Not the Big Ben, crown jewels London, or tourist London, but the real city. I lived in South London. It was Saturday evening and I was out with a friend. I don't remember where we were going, but I remember passing in front of Selhurst train station. As we passed in front of a bus stop, we passed a group of five or six young men. As the last young man passed by, he grabbed me by the collar and said, "Give me your phone!" Street crime and violence was, and still is, common in the real London. It is a part of the city that is not often seen on television. I was never fond of being robbed, and I never learned to back down from a fight. The hilarious thing about the situation was I don't think I even had a phone, and I definitely had no money. Maybe it was partly the sudden adrenaline rush of the situation that placed my thinking on pause. I swung at him, and he slumped over. I put all that I had into that right hook. I was left fighting his friends, and I was severely outnumbered. The use of simple math might have prevented this situation.

I've been knocked out a few times, and each time something weird would happen. This was my first time being knocked unconscious. I don't know how exactly it happened; I just know that somehow I was knocked out. Suddenly, I remember watching myself falling in slow motion from across the street. Where I am from, when someone gets knocked out, they get stomped, but when the lights went out for me in this situation, something strange happened.

As I fell to the ground, I remember looking at the scene from across the street from the train station. The crazy thing about my memory of the situation is it correlates with my friend's accounts of what happened. I watched myself fall to the ground in slow motion, when suddenly my friend Rowlando appeared at the train station doorway. His eyes widened as he saw me, and he did not waste a second. He sprang into action, and behind him followed Jeremy, Javan, and Richard. Before I hit the ground, they intervened in the situation. I hit the ground and bounced back up instantly, ready to fight again. Or so I thought. Rumor is that I was down for a bit. But this is my story and I say I got back up, and I'm sticking to it.

One thing I remember seeing from across the street, was my friend, hiding in the shadows. I had been fighting alone. He could have helped me. He could have been a weapon for my aid, but he chose not to help. I don't know how I have a clear memory of that situation, especially such a clear memory of the scene. I'm pretty sure I was unconscious before I hit the ground. But this situation serves as an illustration for my spirituality today. God is involved in a war today. I am a weapon in this war. I could choose to be a weapon and involve myself in God's controversy like Rowlando and my friends did for me. Or I could silently disappear into the shadows and be safe, as my other friend may have done. I was created to be a weapon used for God. I choose to fight! I refuse to live life the safe way. This situation, along with many others, reminds me that God is watching out for me.

Your body was created perfectly. I hope that you can see from our story about Lucifer what can happen if you get too caught up with yourself. Our perfection comes from our connection with God. That connection makes you a weapon to be used for God. You can prepare to be a weapon by hearing and doing the words of Jesus. Your actions will produce results. If you prepare yourself to be a weapon, others will follow. That is what Jesus is looking for when he comes back. Jesus is not looking for rousing praise, perfect church attendance, or tithe receipts. Jesus is coming back looking for weapons. Will he come back looking for you? I challenge you to go beyond the walls of your church as Jesus did. Do not let God be imprisoned in the weekend. As you do so, you will make plenty of mistakes, but you will learn and you will grow.

Questions for Reflection:

- ✓ How will you be a weapon for God?
- ✓ How will you convert pain into praise?
- ✓ What is the purpose for your existence?
- ✓ Do you choose to fight?
- ✓ What is your purpose?
- ✓ How will you change your world beginning with your mind?
- ✓ What passions do you have?
- ✓ What talents do you have?
- ✓ What changes can you make to focus?
- ✓ How can you convert unpleasant situations?
- ✓ How will you be a weapon?
- ✓ How can you convert pain into praise?

Chapter Six
The Messy Trail

When we fall, we arise stronger people. Thus, there is a blessing when we fall and when we fail. God allows us to be strengthened by our failures. If we can milk our unfortunate situations for growth, we will become, through God, invincible!

We've acknowledged that there may be a problem with our paradigm of church and that we need a change. We talked about how our innate creativity is powered by our connection with God. We've learned to pray about our path forward and invited God to lead our passions. We now see ourselves as weapon. And now the real work shall begin.

Have you ever seen a baby stand up and start sprinting without ever falling? Neither have I. Life is a learning experience, but first we have to take action. Like that baby, we can learn as much, if not more from the times we fall. I know that I grow a lot more from my failures than my successes, and God has blessed me to have survived failure a lot. Converting your pain into passion and passion into praise is a journey. It may not be a straightforward or easy journey. You must be perseverant and keep on until you hear Jesus say, "Well done."

I started college in August of 2003. I was an excited freshman at Oakwood College, now Oakwood University in Huntsville, Alabama. I tried to play it cool, and not to let people know that I was afraid, and that I felt alone. I was being a big boy. I had come straight from London, England. London, England, is very different from Huntsville, Alabama. There have been few moments in my life that I was quiet, but my first few months in Alabama were full of quiet moments. I was surrounded by people with funny dialects. And everything was so… American. I was far from home and I was constantly reminded of it. I was 18 and living away from home, and I left like I was a man. My dream was to graduate college by 21 and to be a successful accountant. My plan was to attend summer school and take extra classes and have my degree knocked out quickly. That was the plan.

Eight years later and I was still in school, studying accounting. I had transferred four times. To be fair, it wasn't my grades. I could not get financial assistance until I had a state of residency. To assist with this, I joined the United States Air Force Reserve, after which Alabama was proud to claim me as a resident. I was accepted at Auburn University in Montgomery. At the same time, I joined Air Force Reserve Officer Training Corps (AFROTC) to train to be an officer. I made the Dean's List and AFROTC invited me to attend Alabama State University to get a full scholarship. I graduated in May of 2012, and was commissioned as an officer in the United States Air Force at the same time. I thank God for not going along with my plan; the divine plan was far better than mine.

My biggest lessons in college were not from the classroom, but from my experiences with failure. I was persistent. Sometimes it's called being stubborn. Sometimes people call it being "hardheaded." But, if you want something, be hardheaded. Delete the word quit from your vocabulary. Do not let the word "can't" roll off your tongue. "Can't" is a lie of Satan's because Jesus said you can. When you fall on life's messy trail, you are in the perfect position to pray. Pray and get back up. Pressure produces diamonds, and fire purifies gold. Tears are fuel to success; please do not waste them. You have to be stubborn enough to know that everything is working out for your good. That is what this chapter is all about, the messy trail of life. We grow the most from our experiences. I would say that unpleasant experiences produce the most growth. At least it has for me.

Sometimes I just sit and think about how my life has flourished. If I had chosen differently, I might not have the privilege of being Salina's annoying husband or Abigail and Grace's crazy dad. I realize throughout all my failures and my disappointments, God was in control of everything in my life the entire time. God allowed my failures; my losses were not really losses. I am not powerful enough to derail God's plan for me. I am exactly where God planned for me to be. You are exactly where God planned for you to be, no matter the situation. These situations sometimes produce the strongest people. God can use the negative and the positive experiences to grow you into the person that he wants you to be. On the messy trail of life, either way, God wins.

When the Trail Gets Unbearable

I'd like to share the stories of a few people who inspired me while I was going through my construction process. I am still in my construction process and I am still being inspired by people and this list continues to grow, but please allow me to share a few.

My friend Obi was an inspiration to many people while at Alabama A&M University. He was from Chicago, and he had endured a rough upbringing. Obi's determination to make it out of Chicago was visible to everyone. He was popular on campus, and known at all the surrounding schools. And when I say popular, I mean there was not a person at Alabama A&M who did not know who Obi was. He was Vice President of Student Government, a member of House Arrest 2, and in Alpha Phi Alpha Fraternity. Obi's determination was unsurpassable, as he always found a way to get things done.

After Obi graduated, he moved to West Virginia for a job. Somehow, he ended up losing the position. Obi had little going for him in West Virginia. Eventually, he became homeless, but did not quit chasing his passion for serving others. He went from living in a homeless shelter to being CEO of a nonprofit to empower young men. His nonprofit was such a huge impact on the youth of his community that it was recognized by the city. Obi's failures and disappointments fueled his fire and we were all proud to know him. Unfortunately, my dear friend was killed in a car crash in 2017. Obi's passing was a shock to everyone. It was as if his memory sparked the fire that set so many on their paths to living each day full out. And although his passing was unfortunate, I am glad to know that he never left God's hand.

Brian Johnson graduated from University of Alabama. Coming out of college, he landed a great job in Atlanta. Brian's friends, family, and his girlfriend considered him a success. Life was good for him in Atlanta. It seemed like all at once Brian's life took a turn. He lost his job, was served an eviction notice, broke up with his girlfriend, and his car was marked for repossession. All these things seemed to happen to him all at once. The pressure was more than he had ever had to handle. When life seemed too unbearable to continue, God used Brian's passion for music to save his life. He told me that he sped down 285 in Atlanta driving over 100 miles per hour contemplating ending his life by crashing, so he could be freed of the pain. The temptation to let go of the wheel at his exit and end it all was real. But as these thoughts raced through his head, the lyrics to Kanye West's "Power" snapped him back to reality. God speaks to us in mysterious ways and he spoke to Brian through Kanye West in his time of need. Brian used this situation as fuel, as motivation to keep going.

Brian is now a successful producer, bestselling author, and an inspirational speaker.[62] Brian helped me to realize that our lives are a culmination of these events that shape us. When I asked what experiences shaped his life, this instance was not one. Brian recalls living with his

---

[62] www.liveyourdreamsoutloud.com

single mother in rural Alabama. His mother had to work multiple jobs and struggle to make ends meet. Brian was influenced by the dedication and perseverance of his mother. Today he is successful, not because of one incident, but a collection of incidents. Brian's experiences could have broken him, but they molded him into the man he is today. Today he inspires and motivates so many, including myself. He is in the position to empower others because God placed him there. God had a plan for Brian just as he has a plan for you and me. God's plan for us is not always straightforward. It definitely wasn't for my boy Marcus.

My boy Marcus discovered his passion for photography at an early age. Marcus is one of those special people whose talent is limitless. After discovering his talent for photography, he began to listen to advice from people. They advised him that photography was a saturated market and that he needed a career that really made money. Marcus began school at Oakwood University in 2003 as an elementary education major. He wanted to teach, or so he thought, until he changed his major to general studies. He started a master's in social work at Alabama A&M University, but he realized that was not what he really wanted to do. Searching for his passion, he opened a martial arts studio, but he found that wasn't it either. He became a Zumba instructor but found that wasn't his passion either. Marcus worked at FedEx while he tried to figure out what he was supposed to do with his life. I told you Marcus could do everything. Thankfully, as of now, Marcus is living out his purpose as a successful photographer, videographer, and entrepreneur. His experience with finding his passion and purpose allows him to connect with people who are going through what he went through. As the CEO of Kreative Marcs Media,[63] Marcus' company does fantastic photography and videography. He ministers as a speaker with I am God's Point of View[64] and he has a phenomenal T-shirt line.[65] I told you he does everything!

---

[63] www.kreativemarcsmedia.com

[64] www.iamgpov.com

[65] www.Isaiah5589.com

Although some of the situations we face in life are unfortunate, we serve a God who is all powerful. God is powerful enough to build our success from our unfortunate situations. Our stupid decisions are not stupid enough when compared to his wisdom. Our most ingenious plan isn't smart enough. The malice of our enemies is not hateful enough when it comes to God's power. There are not enough words in the English language to describe God's power. There is no power in this world that can pry us away from God's will for us, except for ourselves. These situations that we go through may seem tragic to us, but God uses them as character development, as a springboard for his glory just as he did for Joseph in the Bible.

A Story for God's Glory

Joseph was the second youngest of 12 boys. He was his father's favorite, and his father, Jacob, made no secret of it. Jacob made Joseph a coat of many colors, as worn by dignitaries, to show his favor for him. With such open favoritism shown by their father, Joseph was not the favorite of his brothers. Their hate and jealousy led them to sell him into slavery.

Potiphar, the Egyptian, purchased Joseph as a slave. Despite being a slave, Joseph rose to the most trusted position on Potiphar's staff. He was falsely accused by Potiphar's wife and sent to jail. Joseph was pardoned from his alleged crimes and appointed as a leader in Pharaoh's staff in Egypt. From that position, he saved the country and his family from starvation and reunited his family. Joseph's situation was fuel to his fire. God had a plan. He never abandoned Joseph, even when Joseph may have felt like he did. When Joseph was on his death bed, he called his family to him. He said, "You thought evil against me, but God meant to turn it into good."[66] He realized that God was more powerful than any situation he could find himself in.

---

[66] Genesis 50:20

God can use situations that people may have meant for evil for good. Life is uncertain. At times good things will happen and bad things will happen. It is our job as Christians to trust God's process. God's end goal is to take us home to heaven, and that might not include being a millionaire or thriving. We must trust in God's process, even if it is not what we imagine for ourselves. Trust God even when it leads us down a messy trail. Without character-building situations, we would not have the tears to fuel creativity or passion. We'd have no connection with our suffering world. I thank God for my mess. If God can take the pain and the mess of this world and use these situations to refine us, then this world might not be such a cruel place.

The mistakes I made, the times I failed, and the pain that I have experienced have placed me where I am today. I'm not saying I am in the perfect place today, far from it, but I am exactly where God wants me to be. And so are you. There is no better place to be in the world than in God's hands. I feel invincible because I am learning to accept God's plan in my life and see the good in unfortunate situations. I encourage you to try it too. What do you have to lose? Tell your friends about what God has done for you. Create a community to support and share.

Daniel Holder

Questions to Consider:

- ✓ In what situations have you seen God's hand?
- ✓ With what unique demographic does your situation connect you?
- ✓ How have you been strengthened by your situation?
- ✓ How can you be strengthened by your situation?
- ✓ What passions have been revealed by your situations?

Chapter Seven
Alternative Ministers

I therefore (Paul), a prisoner for the Lord, beseech you that you walk worthy of the vocation wherewith ye are called. - Ephesians 4:1 KJV

Paul described Christianity, not as a religion or a belief, but as a vocation. He described Christianity as a job. A job is how you sustain your life. When you think of your Christianity as a vocation, you will get paid. God's payroll is far more reliable and lucrative than your employer's. How can you turn your Christianity into a vocation that you do every day?

Heavenly Misconceptions

Heaven is not going to be as packed as our church services. Jesus said, "Many shall say to me in that day, 'Lord, Lord have we not prophesied in your name, and cast out devils in your name, and done many wonderful works?'"[67] Many of the church members who pack the pews in his name will not even boast these things. To me this verse says that there are many whom we respect as devout Christians whom

---

[67] Matthew 7:22

Jesus does not know. There may be many pastors, bishops, and clergy whom Jesus looks at with unfamiliarity. To these many people, Jesus is going to say, "I don't know you, fam!" I don't want to hear those words, nor do I want any of my friends to hear those words. There are times when I take the Bible literally. Not as much when the Bible says, "Ye shall not destroy the corner of thy beard."[68] My facial hair game isn't strong enough to take that literally. But when the Bible says, "Whatever you do, do it for the glory of God,"[69] I take that literally. I think that doing everything, not just everything on our one worship day, is what will make us more familiar to Jesus.

Our occupations make up so much of what we do. I spend more time at work than I do with my family sometimes. I do not want my identity to be formed by my occupation, and social identity is often defined by our occupation. I'd like to be Daniel, the Christian before I'm Daniel, the project manager. This chapter is not about convincing you to quit your job, unless you want to. Its purpose is to encourage you to think about your purpose. How can you combine the activity you spend the majority of your time doing, with your relationship with God?

Occupation defined social identity, even in Jesus' time. Peter the fisherman, Zaccheus the tax collector, and Jairus the temple leader are some examples. Who I serve should define me. I want the people in my circle to know I am a Christian and I serve God. I want to use my circle of influence to influence people for Jesus. Imagine if service was not associated with church but with Christian individuals. Imagine if you shared Christ, not with words, but with actions. Christ's love is to be *shown* to our friends and loved ones, not told. We shouldn't have to force feed the gospel to people. By showing concern for people and praying for them they will follow our example. Jesus didn't tell people

---

[68] Leviticus 19:27
[69] 1 Corinthians 10:31

to "go and sin no more" until after he had met their need. Ministry is more than an evangelistic series or bringing a friend to church. Ministry is connecting with people to demonstrate to them the love that Jesus has for us.

This book was born from the idea of individual ministry. What if you could be paid to work for Jesus? At my old job, when asked my occupation, I would tell them I was a government-sponsored Bible worker. At work, we hosted a weekly Bible study for the troops. I lived on base and we would pray and study with others that lived and worked there. One morning before dawn, I had devotion on my front porch. A few minutes after I came inside, my doorbell rang. I opened the door and it was a sergeant. She said that she saw me reading my Bible and was inspired to study more and asked me if I would pray with her. We prayed together and talked until dawn. God doesn't wait until normal business hours to work and neither should you. Whatever you do, whether you deliver babies or deliver pizza, how can it be done to the glory of God? I hope that by doing my job, I demonstrated Jesus to somebody. People are always watching.

Attending church teaches one many things. I found that best way to learn something is to teach it to someone else. As a freshman in college, I couldn't afford books. This became a problem for me in my accounting classes. In class, we would work through exercises from the books, and without a book, it was difficult to follow. Fortunately, a lack of resources is the greatest inspiration for creativity. I would offer to tutor my classmates if I could borrow their books for a night. I would figure out how to do the exercises and show others in my class how to do them. I became confident at accounting because I taught others. I'm glad I couldn't afford books. I had to learn not only for myself, but to teach others.

After my successes in class, I applied this same technique to Christianity. I didn't study to learn, I studied to share. God led me into sharing situations and I saw tremendous growth. In this class of Christianity, we all have the textbook — the Bible. We should study to teach and do, not only to know. When we do this, we grow. Unapplied knowledge is foolishness and is soon forgotten. What if we applied the knowledge learned in church to teach others? What would it look like if we did, instead of talking about doing? What would it look like if we focused our Christianity on the activity of six days and not the single day?

Jesus demonstrated the ultimate growth through his experience. Jesus didn't launch ministry by finding promising theologians for his disciples. Jesus came and followed the Old Testament biblical narrative of taking the small insignificant things of this world and defeating mighty things. You can see this concept illustrated in stories like David and Goliath,[70] and the story of Gideon and his small band of men.[71] Jesus chose fishermen to be his followers, men who were despised by the Jews. He chose publicans, and he chose sinners. Through his choice of followers, Jesus was making a point. After three years of being with Jesus, the disciples went on to found the Christian church. Jesus showed them miracles, talked to them, and gave them the opportunity to go out and try these things themselves.[72] Jesus demonstrated that he could change the world using common people. Jesus demonstrates to us that he can use our shortcomings to develop us. Jesus demonstrates that he can make an impact in the world and because of him, we can too.

Let's Make This Practical

Jesus did not live life in a bubble. He was well aware of the things that were going on in his time. He was aware of the beliefs of the different groups. He was aware of the customs, and he demonstrated

---

[70] 1 Samuel 17

[71] Judges 7

[72] Matthew 10

that he was aware of the policies. For example, when he healed 10 lepers, he instructed them to go and show themselves to the priests.[73] A declaration of cleanliness from the leaders was a ticket back into normal society. Jesus was aware of the customs for lepers. Could being familiar with the customs of our community be a start for us? Knowing the struggles of our community is a huge step in connecting with people. You can connect with immigrant Americans by acknowledging that they may feel targeted right now. You can connect with African-Americans by acknowledging that their lives do matter. You can connect with Muslims, Sikhs, and Hindus by acknowledging that they are people, not just the villains that the media portrays. We can connect the sick and families of the sick by acknowledging the epidemic of disease. We can connect with those addicted to alcohol, nicotine, weed, heroin, or Candy Crush by acknowledging that their addiction is real. People suffer from marital problems, depression, and financial instability. These are all opportunities to connect. These are all issues that Christians may face. By acknowledging problems, we show the world that Jesus does care about what they are going through. That's why he sent us, and that is why he allows us to go through problems. Every problem is an opportunity to show someone Jesus.

Jesus went through problems himself. He was an innocent victim of the justice system. Jesus even acknowledged he knew what sins people struggled with when he wrote the sins on the ground.[74] For us, posting people's sins on a bulletin board might be a bad idea. What if instead we held each other accountable. I started a secret group for husbands called "The Fight Club." Even my wife didn't know about it, until now. (Sorry, dear!) "The Fight Club" is an accountability group for men who are intentional about fighting for their marriages. We don't wait for relationship problems to connect. I assume that

---

[73] Luke 17:11-19

[74] John 8:6

marriage is the beginning of all marital problems. "The Fight Club" is a group for husbands to pray together, talk, and share. To me, that is what Christianity is about: being there for your brother by discovering ways to hold each other accountable. In writing this book, I have friends that hold me accountable. Friends don't let friends fail.

Christians have an imaginary bubble that they make to allegedly protect themselves. After baptism, sometimes we are encouraged to stop associating with our non-Christian friends. We replace them with new Christian friends and do Christian activities. This is one of the most detrimental actions we perform that stunts our spiritual growth. We surround ourselves with people that have the same views as us. If we disconnect ourselves from all non-Christian friends, with whom do we share the good news? Who will be positively impacted by the positive changes in our lives? Who will we teach to grow, and who will be an example to? Who will force us into accountability? The Christian bubble is the most detrimental thing to our experience. Challenge strengthens faith. We know what we should and should not do. And if we forget what we should be doing, our friends know and they will remind us. My friends know that I'm a vegetarian, so if they see me with a chicken wing in my hand, they will tell me to put it down, or at least they are supposed to. Friends help friends to succeed.

Let's do our best to pack heaven to its capacity by building a heaven on earth through community. I used to promote parties in college. Although the party community was lit, rarely did anyone wander in because they heard the noise. I had to tell people to come. Most events I had to physically bring people. To get 10 people to come to an event you may have to tell 50. And that was for events that were less than $20. The cover fee for heaven is everything you have; it costs your all to get to heaven. That means that the percentage is going to be far lower. To pack heaven, we must tell everybody. It's going to take all our effort, not one day out of six, but let's work for six days to pack heaven.

By profession, I am a project manager, but I'm a project manager for Jesus, and I want the world to know. Even though you get paid by your employer, let's think of how you can be an undercover agent for Jesus. And let's be sure we do not get "in too deep" like Donnie Brasco. Let's remember our goal and why God placed us in certain positions and around certain people. There is a duality to this Christianity thing. We must work to grow in our social vocations to feed ourselves. The duality is that at the same time, we must work to grow in the spiritual realm and advance the kingdom of heaven. We must not separate the two, but intertwine them, so that when we see growth in one, we may see growth in the other. We are paid to grow in our occupation; let us grow spiritually also. While I cannot offer a blanket formula on how to do this, I do make myself available as a coach.

Let's make our Christianity practical again. Christianity is more than what we talk about at church and at worship. It is about what we do. Let's use our Christianity to attack our community problems and teach other people the love of Jesus and not denominational doctrines. There is a way to connect all of mankind, and that's by showing and giving love. I need for Jesus to know me on that day he speaks of in Matthew 7. I want to hear the words "well done." I work towards that end. By alternative minister, I mean anyone with a vocation, a job, a passion, a talent, a spade, or maybe a pulse can be a minister for God. Whatever it is that you choose to do, do it to the glory of God so that we call can pack heaven.

Alternative Missionaries Throughout History

Deep in the mountains of northern Italy lived a group of wanted criminals. These fugitives took shelter in the mountain caverns. They were proclaimed "heretics" by the Roman Catholic church. When they were captured, they were sometimes killed by being thrown from cliffs. Sometimes whole families were killed in this way. These families were sometimes assassinated, sometimes mutilated, but always hunted. The Roman Catholic church sought to erase their memory from history. Any books that mentioned their existence were committed to flames. These fugitives, the Waldensians, simply believed in the doctrines of the Bible over the word of the Pope. These people, before the invention of the printing press, had copies of the Bible in their native tongue. Their allegiance to the Bible caused them to flee to the mountains. But they did not flee to the mountains to hide. In the majestic mountains, they worshipped together in caves. They trained their youth as missionaries.

As a part of their training, the youth copied the Bible by hand. These youths then reentered society disguised with a trade. Some were students, others were merchants and peddlers. They entered society armed only with the knowledge of scripture. Well, they did carry one weapon. In their clothes, they stitched secret compartments. In these secret compartments, they concealed their most powerful weapon — hand-copied pages from the Bible. They would share these pages with anyone who was interested. The Waldensian youth committed the gospel to memory from childhood. They were trained for mission work. They were sent from their mountain hideouts into the world to spread the good news to everyone. They went out with a purpose armed with a secular trade as a disguise. They were fugitives. But as their trade grew, their spiritual influence grew also.

Today we are not fugitives. Most of us have easy access and open to the scripture. Most of us do not face persecution. Is that the problem? Are we too comfortable with our access? Have we traded mountain caverns for plush churches? Have we traded donkeys for 65-million-dollar jets? Have we gotten too comfortable for our Christianity to be used as God's weapon? How can we refocus and get back to our mission? Jesus said the reason for following him is to become fishers of men.[75] We need to get back to this.

---

[75] Matthew 4:19

When I think of things we can do today to use our talents for the glory of God I think of my friend Jason. Jason grew up in Trinidad and Tobago. He says he never felt poor, but he knew he was not rich. Jason was always good at math and physics, and he knew that those talents were his ticket to doing well in life. Jason studied engineering, but while in grad school, Jason felt a redirection. It's not everyone's calling to leave their job or profession, but for Jason it was. Jason dropped out of graduate school and founded "Pastors Line,"[76] a phenomenal tool to help churches improve their communication. Jason is now an expert in digital communications and CEO of Pastors Line. He directly uses his talents to further the gospel. I mention Jason, not because he is better than anyone else, but because he took the leap of working for himself over working for someone else. Jason uses his talents for God. Every time I talk to Jason I am encouraged by his faith through his entrepreneurial experience. Jason shows me that you can use any talent for ministry. He reminds me that with God there is no limit, and anything is possible. I admire Jason and keep him in my prayers constantly.

Jesus did not hang out in the temple healing whoever came in. Jesus went out and met the people where they were. Jesus demonstrated far more than he preached. He lived with the disciples as he taught them. His patience while teaching was immense. Even after his death, the disciples still did not understand the totality of his mission. Christianity was a movement that was born out of disappointment. The man that they invested their hope in was murdered in the most shameful way imaginable. But that disappointment created a passion that burned inside them — a passion that gave birth to unifying action. Jesus' spirit of change must be revived in us today. God did not create us to exist. He created us to change and influence the world. If we are not being the influence, then we are being influenced. We

---

[76] www.pastorsline.com

can be the salt and light of the world and we don't have to do it alone. Salt changes flavor, and light dispels darkness. We were not created to exist, to survive, or to hold fast. We were created to disturb, dispel, and change!

Can you connect your Christianity with your income? I would love to be paid to work for Jesus. We each have a unique way that we can connect to people and their problems. We can each contribute to converting each problem into an opportunity to show others Jesus. Each field of study or career is different angle in which we can see and connect others to Jesus. I hope that we can all become fishers of people.

Questions to Consider:

- ✓ How can you apply the Bible practically?
- ✓ How can you preach with no words?
- ✓ What can you do in your everyday life?
- ✓ Do you study to teach?
- ✓ Who can you teach?
- ✓ Who is watching you?
- ✓ How can we use our jobs and careers to grow in our religious experience?
- ✓ How can we, following Jesus' example, change our communities and give God the glory?
- ✓ How can we follow Jesus' example today and grow?

Chapter Eight
Creating the World Wide Web

The backbone of Jesus' ministry was his connection with people. There is power when we connect with others. The Bible says, "For where two or three are gathered in my name, there am I in the midst of them."[77] Why not do everything in God's name? Submit all of your connections to his name and live in his presence. Why not create a network of connections to be church together and work for God 24/7?

A Candle on a Hill

When I was younger, whenever I would leave the house my mother would remind me who my heavenly Father was. She would remind me that because of my royalty, people would be watching me. She would whisper in my ear, "Remember, people are watching what you do." I must admit that for my whole life it seems that that has been true. People seem to see my every move, especially when I do things I shouldn't.

While a student at Alabama A&M University, in Normal, Alabama, I had completely strayed away from the Christian ideals

---

[77] Matthew 18:20

my parents had taught me growing up. My friend John and I spent our days there in drunken buffoonery. While enrolled in school, we did all in our power to earn alcohol poisoning, but never got it. There were some nights that we would drink and would not have a clue what happened the next morning. Some mornings we would scrape ourselves up from wherever we awoke. We would reconvene on John's couch in Normal Hills, the student apartments. People would come by the apartment or call and tell us what happened the night before. People were watching us.

Whether you decide to do bad or good, people are watching whether you see them or not. What message would you like to give to those people? There are times when my daughters will use a phrase that we do not like. My wife and I will look at each other with that "Where did she get that from?" look. But we both know, they get it from us. Your children. younger siblings, and relatives are watching you. People at your job or school are watching you. Your life is a spectacle for all to see whether you like it or not. Sorry to say this, but people believe not by what you say, but by what you do. You can choose to be a good influence or a negative influence. I recommend being a positive influence. You speak much louder when you show rather than tell people who you are.

On the other hand, there will be times when you make mistakes, if you're human like I am. When you learn of your mistakes, be humble enough to apologize quickly. There is no way to demonstrate Jesus to someone you may have hurt, until you apologize. Apologize, and apologize quickly.

You are an immense impact to your people around you. You are a candle on a hill so that everyone can see your light. People are watching you, holding you accountable for what you claim. Live your life to be a witness to those people. After all, a light does not shine for itself. A light is a servant; it shines to provide light to those around. Even if you've shown people a poor example of a Christian like I once did, fortunately, God is so forgiving that he remembers only the good we send out. As long as we live, God will never stop forgiving us. Now you have another chance to make things right. People are watching you. It's your job to show them Jesus.

A Profitable Message

The message of Jesus is a magnet to people because it offers genuine hope and help. Jesus demonstrated that the law of the Old Testament was relevant in the situations of his world. Jesus was concerned with the way they were doing church in that day. I am quite sure he would feel the same about how we do church today. The traditional church, the priests, Pharisees, and Sadducees despised Jesus. They contrasted Jesus' ministry. There is a verse in Isaiah that seems to espouse Jesus' ministry. The verse says, "Is not this the fast that I have chosen? To loose the bands of wickedness, to undo the heavy burdens, to let the oppressed go free, and that ye break every yoke? Is it not to deal thy bread to the hungry?"[78] Jesus loosed the bondage of injustice, sickness, and even death. This verse to me gives a synopsis of Jesus' ministry as if he was following these instructions. His message was to help those who needed help.

Jesus said, "Then the King will say to those at his right hand, 'Come, O blessed of my Father, inherit the kingdom prepared for you from the foundation of the world: for I was hungry and you gave me food, I was thirsty and you gave me drink, I was a stranger and you welcomed me, I was naked and you gave me clothing, I was sick and visited me, I was in prison and you came to me."[79] Jesus came to make the same message of the Old Testament personal to us. He intended that we would do these acts in an imitation of him. He also came to

---

[78] Isaiah 58:6-7 KJV
[79] Matthew 25: 34-36 RSV

connect with suffering and reminds us that when we help others, we are helping him. Jesus' message is like a chain. We must connect with others as he connected with us to keep the chain growing.

I'd like to suggest that the message can be monetarily and spiritually profitable. What if our message could be connected to our income? So instead of inviting our friends to attend a church, we should invite them to serve. All over the world there are people that need help. There are huge international organizations known as nonprofit organizations that provide them with help. The leaders of these large organizations sometimes have huge salaries. In a way, they follow the message of Jesus. Often these organizations cause more harm than good. Sometimes cunningly under the guise of helping, they keep people in poverty. Jesus recognizes cunning and he wishes that his followers would execute the same in their work for him.[80]

There is a huge benefit in connecting our income with ministry; however, we must watch that we do not get greedy. We do not need to be business' greatest mind. We could be a tentmaker like Paul. When we give God 100%, we can trust that it will work. To be profitable in the long run, a business must be flexible and able to adapt to market change. In order to face these market changes head on, the gospel message must remain flexible. To maintain this flexibility, it cannot be founded on the building that is the church facility, but on the individual, God's church facility.

But this example is more about than monetary benefit. The return is potentially far more than we could imagine. There are huge spiritual returns should we choose to acknowledge them. Jesus says take no thought for tomorrow and suggests we store up for ourselves treasures in heaven.[81] That was an invitation to us to do some long-term investment. We are offered the opportunity to invest beyond

---

[80] Luke 16:8,9
[81] Matthew 6:17

the few years we will spend in retirement. That invitation still stands. Jesus still invites us to invest in our eternity. As far as I know, no one can take anything with them when they die. When you invest in stocks, bonds, or bitcoin, you can only invest for the length of your lifetime. Some of these investments return dividends to the investors to show gratitude. Imagine how much dividends your Father would pay you for investing in heaven? Even in this, the potential dividends are not the reason for investment. Jesus says, where your treasure is, your heart will be there also.[82] I want to invest in heavenly treasure, and I'd be happy for the earthly dividends. If I seek first the kingdom of God, my other needs will be supplied.[83] But you shouldn't just invest in heaven for the dividends. You should invest in heaven because you want to place your heart there. I want to go home to heaven one day when my work here is complete. We may invest in treasure in heaven by serving God today, as God prepares our homes for us. Yes, the gospel of Jesus is a long-term investment opportunity. Invite your friends to invest with you.

We all have that one friend that wants us to join some business that they have. Today, may I be that friend that invites you into an opportunity? Not to make money but to serve God and allow him to provide for all your needs. The pay on God's payroll is phenomenal. Combine your passion and creativity with his service and be a full-time minister at whatever you do. Give your talents to God and see them multiplied.

The purpose of Jesus' message was to connect with others. Connect, glorify God, be the church, and spread God's love. Make a full-time occupation out of spreading his love in whatever way God has created you to do so. Please invite your friends to join you and create a network of friends. Glorify God together with your passions

---

[82] Matthew 6:21
[83] Matthew 6:33

and support each other. God can use you and provide for your needs. He has enough to provide for your friends too!

It's All About the Fruit

A sickle is a short farming tool with a semicircular blade used for harvesting. A harvest signifies an end to labor. No more plowing, weeding, watering, or picking, the harvest is time to celebrate. It is the imagery of a harvest that is used in the Bible to describe the return of Jesus. It is no coincidence that Jesus is pictured with a sharp sickle in his hand[84] in one text. Jesus is ready to call for an end to the labor — it's time to eat. This whole debacle is all about fruit. Jesus wants to take the fruit that is ready home with him to heaven. Jesus said, "Every tree that doesn't bring forth good fruit will be hewn down and cast into the fire."[85] He was so angry at a fig tree, for not having figs on it, that he cursed it.[86] Jesus was serious about his fruit. This means that he is serious about you.

Life is a growth experience, and while we are growing, like fruit, we are to grow into trees that will bear fruit. The Bible often describes people as the fruit of the womb.[87] That is the fruit that Jesus is looking for, the fruit of the womb, other people who will grow and bear more fruit. You encounter people every day. The network of people that each one of us know is unique. God is calling you to use your network and be church. As you work, expand your network. Create a worldwide web of people who fish for men.

I guess I'm caught. This is a business opportunity I am offering. I invite you not to be a leader in a church, but the leader of a church. Jesus knew that his church would be in the state it's in today. He

---

[84] Revelation 14:16

[85] Matthew 7:19

[86] Matthew 21:19 KJV

[87] Psalm 127:3

once said, "The harvest is plentiful, but the laborers are few."[88] Jesus needs leaders to labor today. Jesus invites you to labor with him as the church and lead others to be the church also. Create a network of friends to be candles on the hill in your community. In today's atmosphere you are living on a dry hill. The love has gone and greed and corruption have taken over. In a land where the love is gone and corruption and injustice have taken over, your small candle on a hill is dangerous; that candle is likely to cause a brush fire.

I currently live in Southern California. I often see the mountains glowing orange from the blaze, and the planes circling to extinguish the fire. That to me is the image of Christianity, and I'd like to encourage you to be that candle on the hill that could set the whole mountain on fire. Be an intense fire and don't let anyone put you out. If you will be the fire, there is nothing that can extinguish your passion. Be a fire, and set your world ablaze!

Don't be confined to a box. Step out and join or create a community aimed at being vocationally Christian, or alternative ministers. Get some support. Connect with people and connect them with God, as they turn their passion into praise. Show people that it's possible to be vocationally Christian. Apply the knowledge you learn in church, because unapplied knowledge is foolishness. You are the best in the world at being you; the world already has plenty of other people. The world needs you!

---

[88] Luke 10:2 KJV

Daniel Holder

Questions to Consider:

- ✓ How can you use your experience to inspire others to serve?
- ✓ How can you convince friends not to just attend church but to serve?
- ✓ How can you encourage others to be practical with their Christianity?

Conclusion

We've seen examples with the growth of technology that an organization that does not change will die. There is a need for change in church, to keep the message of the love of Jesus flowing. It's time for us to be real with ourselves. We have to question our intentions, motives and actions like never before. We have to know if we are being as faithful as we can be to the mission and the assignment that God has called us to as Christians. God has called each of us to show gratitude to our creator by showing ourselves to be faithful by working for God in everything we do.

This book is a call to action. I implore you to use your passion, your creativity and whatever else you have to glorify God. Give your 100% at whatever it is that you do and live for God. Be a conduit for God's love by following the example of Jesus. Ministry must become what we do seven days a week no matter our occupation. It is time for us to think of ministry, not as a side job, or an obligation for church. We must incorporate ministry into our professions, careers, and entrepreneurial endeavors. I cannot advise you in any particular direction, and if I did advise you, you shouldn't listen. God created each of us with a purpose and a path. I will share how I am seeking to convert my passion into praise. However, we must be sure that we are connected to God through prayer to ensure we are doing the right thing. Sometimes, when we are connected in prayer, we will make mistakes, but remember, life is about growth. When you make mistakes, you also grow.

My dad once warned me, "Be careful who you share what you are doing in faith with because faith seems like foolishness to most people." Today, I'm going to look foolish because I think outside of the box.

It was 2015. I was serving in the United States Air Force as a project manager with a special unit of officers. One day the Lieutenant Colonel called all of the lieutenants into his office. He is standing by his white board and he draws a square. He says, "This is a box. I need for you all to start thinking outside of this box!" He noticed me fidgeting on the other side of the office and says, "Except for you, Holder!" He paused and drew a tiny square in the top left corner of his original square. "Holder, this is your box, don't think outside that box!" I am an outside-of-the-box thinker; furthermore, I don't believe in a box. The box is a figment of imagination created by society. In 2016, I left my career in the United States Air Force to study for ministry, which I was warned against doing. Now I am pursuing my Master of Divinity degree. I have a crazy idea for a church that is not dependent on giving to sustain.

Our communities are filled with so much talent, passion, and experience. I'd love to build a model of a church that is open seven days a week, working and interacting with the community to provide jobs. Our churches, with the correct leadership, are full of the energy and the passion needed to sustain a model like this. Just because I am not a pastor and I do not have a church, that is not going to stop me from building. I dream of a worldwide community where the members support, encourage, pray for, and empower each other to turn passion into praise. There are so many entrepreneurs, musicians, artists, bloggers, coaches, independent ministries, and exceptional people with talents that need a community like this. In this community we will practically apply following Christ. There is something in you that the world needs and if you haven't already found it. I encourage you to discover it. I encourage you to discover how it can be used for God's glory. I'm not suggesting that anyone wait on church to do something. The church is waiting on you. You are church.

This book has been about the world's finest leader — Jesus. Jesus has left more of an impact on the world than any other leader in history. Jesus was a leader who called, inspired, trained and deployed leaders who went forth to change the world. Jesus was a revolutionary. He led a revolution that changed the way people worshipped around the world. Can we go back to that? Can we refocus on Jesus' ministry? Unless we are perfect, that refocus will result in a change. I am positive that it would result in a revolution of the way we worship God today. Our worship would not be based upon the activity of one location, but we would worship God in spirit and in truth, every day. I am positive that we would not only worship God with our words, but the word would result in action. I am certain that those actions would yield results, and those results would change our world. I pray that those results will change our world. More importantly, I pray that those actions will change us.

Compassion moved Jesus as he looked upon the multitude.[89] I don't know how the disciples could tell. His expression may have spilled the beans or possibly a single tear fell from his eye. The disciples knew that his concern was the people with no leaders. Would Jesus have the same look of compassion and concern looking upon the church today? Do we give Jesus the same haphazard impression? Would he see lots of programs, with no real direction, or growth? Would he see lots of tithe giving, but no surrender? Would Jesus see lots of sacrifices, but no real sacrifice? Would Jesus have the same compassion and concern looking at your church? After taking in the scene of the multitude Jesus said, "The harvest truly is plenteous but the laborers are few; pray ye therefore the Lord of the harvest, that he will send forth

---

[89] Matthew 9:36-38

laborers into his harvest."[90] I pray that he has sent forth laborers. I am thankful God sent you because you are church.

This book is not about working to earn heaven or scaring you into working. Connecting with people and working of itself does nothing for a person. The purpose of working is to gain a more intimate connection with God. The purpose of applying your Christian knowledge to your activity of six days a week is to make your Christianity practical and not theory. Knowledge that is not applied is foolishness. How can we create a community that applies our knowledge and grows us in our Christianity? As a Christian community we need unity. We must support, pray for, and encourage one another. The early church was a community, and that community is what the apostle Paul sought. He said:

> "Fulfil ye my joy, that ye be likeminded, having the same love, being of one accord, of one mind. Let nothing be done through strife or vainglory; but in lowliness of mind let each esteem other better than themselves. Look not every man on his own things but every man also on the things of others. Let this mind be in you, which was also in Christ Jesus:"[91]

The Bible implores us so many times to strive for unity of mind. We can do that with the single doctrine of loving others. If we do not seek our own good or our own vanity, we can depend on God to provide for us. The world has enough verbal sermons. Let's have some sermons that are demonstrated through action. The world needs these sermons because that is how they will believe. Let us show people Jesus, not because we have to, but because we love them enough to do

---

[90] Matthew 9: 36,37
[91] Philippians 2:2-5 KJV

so. I invite you to start your own community of people who will turn passion into praise. Develop your own community that will provide support, prayer, and encouragement. Reach out to me. I'm glad to help. Connect with our larger network and let us praise together.

We as Christians are called to be excellent in this world, but we are also called to advance God's kingdom. Christianity is a vocation,[92] not a weekend activity. Work and church are not separate things. Do not separate the two. Allow them to grow together. You are the best in the world at being you. You are exactly what the world needs. You are exactly what the kingdom of heaven needs. I invite you to surrender your life to God. Let's watch the growth. Let's journey together. You are a citizen of heaven. As a citizen of heaven, God gives you permission to go forward with power. The Bible says that the kingdom of God is not in word but in power.[93] We are told that God has not given us the spirit of fear, but the spirit of power and of love and of a sound mind.[94] You have permission to move with power. Jesus moved in the same way. He moved with power and he was enthusiastic. His disciples looked at him in one situation, and remembered where it was written in Psalms, "the zeal of Your house has eaten me up."[95] They could see the passion and the power in Jesus. Let people see the passion and power in you. Be consumed by it.

Your experience, your pain, your passion, and your mistakes have made you into who you are today. You are a finely tuned individual that can never be duplicated. There is no one in the history of the world that can be you like you can be you. Like the master in the parable of the talents, God has left you with a unique set of talents that cannot be duplicated. What will you do with them? How will you use what God has given you? How will you turn your passion into

---

[92] Ephesians 4:1

[93] 1 Corinthians 4:20

[94] 2 Timothy 1:7

[95] Psalm 69:9

praise? If pain turns into passion, when we turn our passion into praise we transform the world from a world full of pain into a world of praise. We will show the world Jesus. How will you show your world Jesus? God did not create the church organization to show the world Jesus. He created you! You are church!

Jesus said, "Blessed are the poor in spirit, for theirs is the Kingdom of Heaven."[96] The Kingdom of Heaven belongs to those who go through pain and feel down. Jesus said this because people who are poor in spirit have a secret weapon. They have pain. There is no greater driver or motivator than pain. When that pain is converted to passion and that passion into praise, there is nothing that can match its intensity. He continued to say that there is a blessing for those that mourn.[97] Jesus taught us how to turn pain into praise with his words, and he demonstrated it with his actions. Now it's our turn. I invite you to connect with me, I'd love to share in your experiences of church and of converting passion into praise.

Look around. Can you see people watching you? What you do is seen by so many. Your actions are a sermon that speak far louder than any words. The sound of words will die out with the sound waves, but your actions make history. Let's make history together, turning passion into praise. Let's step out of the box that doesn't exist and quit doing church normally. It's time to grow into citizens of heaven.

Questions to Consider:

- ✓ How can we be united in love for others?
- ✓ How can we create a network of coworkers who will seek the same growth and the same glory for God?
- ✓ Take an inventory of talents. What makes you unique?

---

[96] Matthew 5:3
[97] Matthew 5:4

Epilogue

Five years ago I spent the summer at home in London, England, with my dad. He was finishing his book, *The Olympic Christian*. On the journey home, I read his first book, *The Power of a Double Portion*. It was about Elijah and Elisha, and the double portion Elisha requested upon Elijah's departure. It was my dad who inspired me to write and realize it was possible. I was able to celebrate his successes but also witness and learn from his pitfalls. My dad, Pastor Richard Holder, opened my eyes to possibilities in writing and entrepreneurship. I learned from his mistakes and I celebrate his successes. My dad provided me with a head start — a head start that I aim to provide to my children.

I wrote this book about converting pain into passion and passion into praise. I tried to write it from the outside, referring to your pain. But God had different plans for me. I gave my mom my manuscript for my book to get her opinion. She read it, liked it, and encouraged me to keep working. I had sent my children to my mom's house for them to spend time with her over Christmas. To be honest, I wasn't going to send them but my wife, Salina, insisted. In January, my mom brought my kids back. On the day we were supposed to pick them up from the airport, someone rear-ended my wife. Salina and I spent a few weeks with both of our mothers and the girls. We enjoyed our time together, walking, talking, cooking, and eating.

My mom left on January 19th, and we celebrated her 61st birthday before she left. My mom reads her Bible every year, and this year marked 45 times she had read her Bible through. After she left, my car was totaled. The next week I was asked to resign from my job or they would seek to fire me. It was unfair, but I chose to leave with my reputation intact. Two weeks later my mom was taken into the hospital with pneumonia and passed away the next day.

On the plane traveling to arrange the funeral, I thought about this book. I had been writing about turning pain into passion and passion into praise, but I had been given a real lesson in it. I talked about growing from unfortunate situations. In my mind this situation tested the validity of this book. I had to believe that my situation was a part of God's plan for me and for my mom. Even though I lost my car, I didn't have to pay my car note. I lost my job, and I had more time to focus on what God wanted from me. I lost my....well, I didn't lose my mother; she was in God's hands. My mother had finished her race. I will miss her, but I'm happy for her. Together, we celebrate her life, which was an amazing one.

We live in a cruel world. The main currency is pain and unfortunate situations. These situations discourage and break people. If you can learn and grow from unfortunate situations and praise God while going through them, you will be invincible. I praise God for my situation, because I want to be invincible. I want you to be invincible too. My main source of encouragement came from my mom via my daughters. My daughters had just spent time with my mom over Christmas, so I wondered how they would take seeing her lifeless in a box at the funeral. Grace looked me in my eye and said, "Daddy, you need to go and give your mommy a hug!" I said "Grace, I can't because the box is in the way. Can I touch her hand?" Abigail interjected, "We want to touch her hand with you!" I conceded, and took their hands and walked the long way around to the casket. Abigail said, "Daddy when we finish, let's go pray." "Yes Abigail," I said. We touched Grandma's hand and proceeded to the back of the church to pray together. I decided to ask them questions to see how they understood the situation and got a shock.

I said, "Girls, what's grandma doing right now?" Grace said, "She's sleeping, waiting for Jesus to wake her up?" I said, "Grace, what's Jesus going to do?" Grace said, "Jesus is going to blow the horn really loud." Abigail interrupted again, "And Jesus is going to take her to heaven!" The next day at family worship I asked them to repeat what they told me, and they did. Abigail added, "I have an idea! We should all go to heaven and hide under blankets. And when Grandma comes there, we should all jump out and yell surprise!" I told Abigail, "That's an awesome idea!" I plan to do just that. However, I think when we all make it there, we might forget about the blankets.

About the Author

Daniel Holder is an author, speaker, and ministry consultant on a mission to draw people closer to God by shattering the stifling traditions of religion, and inciting real change in the heart of the church.

Born and raised in London, England as the son of Pastor Richard and Pennie Holder, Daniel's path to discovering his identity in Christ wasn't a smooth one. After leaving home at the age of 18 to attend college in the United States, he began to make poor choices that included heavy drinking, an arrest, and other reckless behaviors that sent him on a downward spiral. That downward spiral led to the revealing of his purpose and his passion.

Daniel, his wife Salina, and their two daughters, Abigail and Grace, reside in Southern California, where he is currently pursuing a Master's in divinity at La Sierra University. An unconventional and creative thinker, Daniel is dedicated to disrupting ministry as usual and is dedicated to become an agent of change in the church and beyond.

Printed in the United States
By Bookmasters